Sovereigns

PEACEFULLY

Take Charge

SOVEREIGNS - PEACEFULLY - TAKE CHARGE

An Agenda for Liberty and Justice

Allan Matthews

SOVEREIGN PEOPLE PRESS
Reston, Virginia

ACKNOWLEDGMENTS

Review of the manuscript and suggestions for improvement by Doris Haigneré Matthews are acknowledged and deeply appreciated. Artist William Jensen created the front cover and page designs.

The author feels special obligations to the insights, writings, and actions of A. Powell Davies, Martin Luther King Jr., Clarence Streit, Ira Glasser, Jeremy Stone, Ralph Nader, Edmund Morgan, Samuel Beer, Frances Moore Lappé, Lester Brown, and Ruth Leger Sivard.

Library of Congress Catalog Card Number: 96-092954
ISBN Number 0-9655953-0-7

For Kim and David

CONTENTS

TABLES

Page

FIGURES

LIST OF GRIEVANCES AND PROPOSED
CONSTITUTIONAL AMENDMENTS

PROLOGUE AND EIGHT-STEP AGENDA

Most people in the world are discontent. They believe things could be appreciably better for everyone. Yet they haven't figured out just what to do. The basic problem – seldom recognized – is that representative government is not working anywhere on earth. Representative government either does not exist at all, or it operates well below any reasonable level of expected performance in faithfully carrying out the wishes of the people. Both the elite and average people are responsible for this colossal mismanagement.

The elite are to blame because their pride, social habits, and institutions keep them walled off from, and ignorant of, the only comprehensive source of information about the public good – the people as a whole. The people, on the other hand, have allowed representative government to fail by not recognizing their own personal birthright sovereignty and by neglecting to find a way sufficiently to exercise that sovereignty to instruct governments.

So what can we do. Some individuals raise worthy banners. Yet it is unlikely that the elite as a group can be counted on to lead toward effective remedy. For one thing, it is discouraging to note that there has never been demonstrated much correlation between IQ and morality or between eminence and humanitarianism. Even more telling, it is well known that power and prestige seldom listen to the people and almost never voluntarily relinquish dominance. As the elite is not taking appreciable initiatives toward more fairness, we must grasp the root alternative to set a true course toward egalitarianism. It is up to the people. Sovereigns – peacefully – take charge!

The way the people can take charge – outside of government organizations and the market – is to dialogue in town meetings, elect representatives to special constitutional conventions, and to legalize through ratification major reforms and more specific details in written constitutions instructing governments. A proposed agenda for the people to do this, in eight steps, is presented in the following paragraphs. It speaks to people worldwide, but those in the United States, Canada, and Western Europe are best positioned to consider and act on it first.

EIGHT–STEP THREE–YEAR AGENDA

1. For one year, town meetings dialogue on five topics – political, social, and economic grievances (discussed here in Chapter 1), locus of sovereignty (Chapter 2), civil society outside of government and marketplace (Chapter 3), the social contract (Chapter 4), and initiative, referendum, and the proper role of business corporations (Chapter 5). Thereafter the people can elect delegates to separate national constitutional conventions.

2. During the second year, the convention – partly on the basis of town meeting reports – can draft a Declaration of Sovereignty, Rights, and Responsibilities (Chapter 4) and draft constitutional amendments shifting political power. These principally would enable lawmaking by national initiative and referendums and reduce the powers of corporations and issue revised instructions to them (Chapter 5).

3. The people by national referendums can vote on the convention drafts.

4. Meanwhile, during the second year, town meetings can dialogue on four new topics – national powers redelegated to states and communities (Chapter 6), national powers redelegated to a North Atlantic transnational government (Chapter 7), reform of the U. S., Canadian, and Western European constitutions (Chapter 8), and reform of the the United Nations (Chapter 9).

5. During the third year, the constitutional conventions can reconvene and – partly on the basis of town meeting reports – propose (a) a transnational North Atlantic constitutional assembly at Reykjavik, Iceland, and a North Atlantic constitution for the

Eight–Step Three–Year Agenda

1997

Step	Town Meeting	Electorate	National Convention
1	Dialogue: grievances (Ch. 1) sovereignty (Ch. 2) organize civil society (Ch. 3) social contract (Ch. 4) initiative, referendum, business corp. (Ch. 5)	Choose delegates to national constitutional convention	

1998

Step	Town Meeting	Electorate	National Convention
2			Draft declaration (Ch. 4) and amendments on referendums and corp.(Ch. 5)
3		Referendums on convention drafts	
4	Dialogue: decentralization (Ch. 6) transnational (Ch. 7) reform national (Ch. 8) reform U. N. (Ch. 9)		

1999

Step	Town Meeting	Electorate	National Convention
5			Propose N. Atlantic assembly. Draft national and transnational amendments and new U. N. treaty
6		Referendum on 3 convention drafts	
7			Reform U. N.
8	Dialogue: Fairer world (Ch. 10)		

peoples of Western Europe and northern America, (b) amendments to reform national constitutions, and (c) a revised United Nations treaty to be transmitted to the executives of each Western European and northern American nation for consideration.

6. The people by national referendums can vote on the North Atlantic constitution and on amendments to their national constitutions.

7. The national executives of Western Europe and northern America can consider a revised United Nations treaty, consult with representatives of other members of the United Nations, and – if they approve – submit the new treaty to their legislatures for ratification. If citizens do not like the way national governments have acted, or not acted, to improve the the United Nations treaty, they may bypass their national governments and take up the matter by citizen initiative and referendum.

8. In the third year, town meetings might address any and all international issues pertaining to a fairer world (Chapter 10).

This book presents, as one person's opinions, what the constitutional reforms should be and what agenda and procedures to put them into effect. If the book inspires other sovereigns to formulate their own value system and political action – even if quite different from the author's – it will have achieved its purpose.

PART I

WE, THE SOVEREIGN PEOPLE

1

DECLARATION OF GRIEVANCES

Representative government is not working in the United States – or anywhere else. The fundamental defect is that policies in all governments are usually shaped by and for usurping minorities and only occasionally reflect the will of the citizen majority. The principal abuses by government – either directly or through collaborating business corporations – are denial of certain human rights, corrupt election financing, overmilitarization, unfair distribution of income and wealth, unrepresentative upper legislative chambers, excessive allowances of environmental pollution, and reckless stewardship of natural resources.

The failure of government to be representative is due primarily to the absence of sufficiently instructive constitutions ordained and frequently updated by the people. The practices of liberty, justice, and government are fundamentally flawed in the United States because the people who legalized (ratified) its original constitution thereafter – either themselves or their descendants – have failed to this day to uphold their sovereignty and have defaulted to state and national legislatures the essential function of proposing amendments to improve their constitutions. A most damaging and ridiculous interpretation of the U. S. constitution occurred when the Supreme Court ruled in 1886 that a business corporation was a person and entitled to the rights of a person.

It follows that the only way for the government of the United States to become truly representative is major reform of the constitution. Two centuries of experience proves that the government – legislature, executive, and judiciary – cannot adequately reform itself. This is because elections – heavily influenced by money and discriminatory procedures – are corrupt. The people can repossess their government only by reaffirming their sovereignty and taking all the steps – from proposal to ratification – to basically reform the constitution. The amendments would follow from – and be responsive to – justifiable grievances. Thus the process of reform logically begins with a declaration of grievances.

It is difficult to identify and define accurately the political, social, and economic grievances of the majority and at the same time give due weight to the rights of all individuals and minorities. The grievances about to be specified are those of the author. He hopes they may be a pattern in the sense of coinciding with the present or latent grievances of the majority of his associates on earth. At the end of each stated grievance is an assigned number corresponding to numbered remedial constitutional amendments proposed in later chapters of this book.

GRIEVANCES

Incomplete Democracy

- The executive veto and constitutional amendment are not sufficient remedies for the people to overrule Congress and state legislatures when legislators take action – or fail to take action – against the will of the citizen majority (1).

Corporation Defects

- Many corporations are trusts which obstruct competition, block unionization, exploit foreigners with practices illegal in the United States, exert undue influence on legislators, and are deceptive in contract negotiations (2).
- Corporations were outrageously given the rights of persons by the U. S. Supreme Court (3).
- Certain business corporations are too large to be consistent with democracy (4).
- Directors of business corporations represent only one minor section of society – stockholders – and in corporate decision-making undemocratically have their votes weighted by amount of stock possessed (5).
- Corporation money corrupts political elections (6).
- Corporation money corrupts the actions of political candidates and officeholders (7).

Overcentralization
- Bureaucracy at the national level is too centralized and distant from the people. This diminishes the quality and effectiveness of public programs in health, education, social services, public safety, housing, and public works (8).

World Anarchy
- The people of the world continue to be exposed to wars, poverty, and environmental degradation largely because there are no transnational laws to limit the aggressions, injustices, and degradations committed by national governments "in the national interest." Treaties such as NATO and the United Nations are insufficient and undependable (9).

Abridged Human Rights
- Pressures to privatize Social Security are being exerted by insurance companies, bankers, the Cato Institute, and others. (see Eric Laursen) (10).
- In employment selection, setting pay rates, promotions, educational admissions, and insurance rates, there is frequent discrimination against women, racial and ethnic minorities, homosexuals, and aliens. Such discrimination in voter registration, credit, housing, public accommodations, education, and employment in the past has produced unfairness in the present which can be equalized only by affirmative action and other means. Recruiting by word of mouth often restricts applicants to social circles of current employees, notes Kathy Bryan. University registrars usually go beyond merit (test scores and grades) to consider geography, personality, and relationship to alumni or donors in granting admission and thus have no basis for not also considering affirmative action (11).
- Pressures are constantly applied by certain religious adherents to breach the constitutionally mandated separation of church and state. Some government agencies, especially at the local level, have yielded to a wrongful degree (12).
- Crimes committed by Americans are sometimes not a crime under U. S. law if committed outside the U. S. (13).

- Thirty–six states and the national government, after certain court trials, condemn citizens to death and kill them. Retired U. S. Supreme Court Justice William J. Brennan Jr. calls this "barbaric and inhuman punishment that violates our Constitution . . . . The state does not honor the victim by emulating the murderer who took the victim's life." Massachusetts Chief Justice Paul Liacos judges that the death sentence is "torture in the guise of civilized business." (14)

- About a third of persons who are ill in the United States do not have adequate medical care, principally because they do not have enough money to buy it. Some 40 million Americans have no health insurance (15).

- It is believed by some that the people as a civil society are not qualified to govern or to guide government. Yet Thomas Jefferson believed, "I know no safe depository of the ultimate powers of the society but the people themselves. And if we think them not enlightened enough to exercise their control with a wholesome discretion, the remedy is not to take it from them, but to educate their discretion." Some parents have become discouraged about community schools; they need to be persuaded to become partners in improving public schools available to all (16).

- Over 35,000 persons are killed in the United States annually by guns. A gun in a house is 27 times more likely to be used in accidental shooting, intentional shooting of a family member, or suicide than against an intruder (17).

- Unsolicited commercial telephone and electronic calls are a nuisance and invasion of privacy. Telemarketers make over 2 million calls to Americans every day (18).

- All laws about abortion are usurpation of personal rights (19).

- Although the right of counsel for defense is guaranteed constitutionally in major criminal cases, such counsel is not guaranteed in civil cases. The Legal Services Corporation, established to assist in this matter, has been limited in functions and in funds by irresponsible Congresses. As regards criminal cases, an unfairness is that the toughest sentences are now "applied to basically one group of people: poor minority people," who are not well connected or do not have attorneys capable of making a deal that "finesses the rules," according to U. S. District Judge Terry Hatter of Los Angeles (20).

- Sometimes when a person or corporation is convicted of a law violation, the records of the court proceedings are sealed and the public is thereby denied detailed knowledge of the wrong-doing (21).
- Efforts are frequently made to impose censorship on the basis of vague, imprecise, or unwarranted terms such as "indecent," "patently offensive," and "unsuitable for children" (22).

Abridged Employee Rights
- Corporations frequently interfere with and penalize the right of workers to organize trade unions. Some 30 million private–sector workers who are not now union members would like union representation, according to David Gordon (23).
- Thirty–six million people were living in the U. S. in 1995 below the poverty level ($15,000 for a family of four), according to the Bureau of the Census. One third of the total population did not have enough income to meet human needs and was distressfully deprived. A manifestation of this is that the poorest fifth of U. S. people have only 4 percent of the total U. S. income, whereas the top fifth enjoy 49 percent of it. "For much of its history, America has been waging war against many of its poor people," says Herbert Gans. "It is a war," he continues, "waged with a variety of weapons, such as withholding the opportunities for decent jobs, schools, housing, and the necessities required for a modest version of the American way of life . . . . The leaders of this war continue to decrease the welfare benefits that go to the poor mothers unable to work or find jobs, threaten to end welfare altogether, increase the punitive conditions under which all help is given, and fan further the hatred of the poor among the more fortunate classes" (24).
- Although a meaningful remunerative job is a personal and family right, 30 percent of the world's labor force is unemployed, according to the International Labour Organization. That per-centage applies even to the U. S., states Lester Thurow, if

calculations are comprehensive enough to include all those wanting work and part–time employees wanting full–time work (25).

- The present 40–hour standard work week appears to be inconsis-
tent with full employment. So that week should be shortened to
distribute work opportunities fairly. Most workers would prefer a
shorter work week to release time for more recreation and other
pursuits (26).

- Congress has established standards for health and safety in the
workplace, but they are frequently not met, and little or nothing
is done about violations, says James Weinstein. This is largely
because governments are unable to monitor many of the 7 million workplaces (27).

Voting Irregularities

- States frequently make voting registration difficult and set the
date of voting on inconvenient work days (28).

- Candidates for political office are very unequal as to availability
of funds for advertising and for other promotions affecting the
outcome of elections (29).

- Allowing each state to have two Senators, regardless of number
of citizens, is undemocratic (30).

- Granting all seats in legislatures to those with a majority of
votes, in a winner–take–all procedure, leaves minorities under-
represented. As a result, "The American election system is
unfair, outmoded, and undemocratic," says Douglas Amy.
Germany, Italy, and nations in Scandinavia, Iberia, and Central
Europe have corrected this by adopting proportional representation (31).

- United States citizens in the District of Columbia and Puerto
Rico suffer taxation without full and equal representation (32).

The Congress

- Members of Congress improperly filibuster (33), divert time
away from national issues to service individuals and organizations (34), accept outside income from individuals and
organizations expecting legislative favors (35), and after their
service in Congress, often lobby Congress for pay (36).

The Presidency
- The Electoral College device of electing the president and vice-president was called "an American political curiosity" by Harry Louis Selden. "It is pure luck that keeps things from going awry under what is at best a caricature of democratic process," he added (37).
- Presidents of the United States have unconstitutionally made war against Viet-Nam, Cambodia, Korea, Cuba, Nicaragua, Granada, Libya, Iraq, and other nations. Those who supported U. S. fighting in Viet-Nam owe confessions of error and expressions of sorrow to the Vietnamese, Americans, and others killed or harmed (38).
- There are occasions when the President and Congressional majorities would like to enact appropriation and other bills without the irrelevant special-interest riders sometimes attached. The Congress and President took a step to address that problem when in 1996 they provided for a line-item veto capability starting January 1997. However, Congress can suspend application of that authority to any legislation any time it wishes. Only a constitutional amendment could prevent such suspensions (39).

Overmilitarization
- Military expenditures by the United States and by NATO are currently four times and seven times, respectively, as great as expenditures by the combined potential adversaries – China, Russia, North Korea, Iran, Iraq, and Libya, according to Ruth Leger Sivard. At least a third of the U. S. military expenditure is useless surplus or unnecessary updating. President Dwight Eisenhower warned that such excess could destroy from within what is trying to be defended from without (40).
- The United States provoked the runaway nuclear arms race with the USSR. During the entire cold-war period the U. S. refused to accept parity of nuclear weapons at a reasonably low level and instead churned out irrational numbers of weapons, consistently adding about 2,000 nuclear warheads to whatever the Soviets produced. Production of nuclear weapons and power has never adequately taken into account the unavailability of a method or

practice for safely disposing of nuclear waste. The number of nuclear weapons still in existence is immensely and dangerously in excess of any rational security need (41).

Environmental Degradation and Resources Waste
- Pollution is excessive, degrading the environment, and often not paid for by the polluter (42).
- Governments are giving away or selling at cheap prices public lands, timber, minerals, and other resources (43, 44).
- Animals are being unduly harmed, often cruelly (45).

Property Responsibilities
- The richest 1 percent of United States families own 40 percent of family wealth, the richest 20 percent own 85 percent, and the bottom 80 percent of families have only 15 percent. Between 1983 and 1989 the top 20 percent of wealth holders received 99 percent of the gain in national wealth, according to Edward Wolff. Germany, Scandinavia, the Netherlands, and Switzerland are among countries with a wealth tax to contribute toward equity. (46).
- Property owners are often shamelessly demanding payment from the public for their inconvenience in obeying conservation, health, and safety laws (47).
- Some owners of seacoast property improperly claim ownership of the land between low tide and high tide (48).

Unethical Business Practices
- An estimated $150 billion a year in direct subsidies and tax breaks – "corporate welfare" – is funneled by Congress to business companies, according to journalist Charles Sennott. That amount is larger than either the annual federal budget deficit or federal social welfare (excluding Social Security and medical care), he adds. (49).
- Many financial practices are secretive, undertaxed, and involve unwarranted public bail–out of private losses (50).
- Business, with collusion of Congress, has usurped the airwaves belonging to the people (51), unwarrantably patented forms of

life (52), uses government espionage for private profit (53), and pays its officers excessive salaries. In some cases pointed out by Ruth Leger Sivard, earnings of corporation executives averaged 190 times the average earnings of their workers (54).

Unfair Foreign Relations

- The World Bank and International Monetary Fund, although sometimes contributing positively to international development, have placed self-serving onerous conditions on loan offers and are conducting "structural adjustment programs" which, in the words of Tony Clarke, "have become instruments for the recolonialization of many developing countries in the South." The harmful measures he refers to include "large scale deregulation, privatization, currency devaluation, social spending cuts, lower corporate taxes, expanding exports of natural resources and agricultural products and removal of foreign investment restrictions." These are discussed in the book edited by Kevin Danaher (55).
- The United States is a backslider in paying its fair share of United Nations expenses (56).
- The U. S. Central Intelligence Agency participated substantially and secretly in the overthrow of elected Mossadegh in Iran in 1953, President Arbenz in Guatemala in 1954, and others. President Harry Truman said in 1963: "I never had any thought that when I set up the CIA that it would be injected into peacetime cloak and dagger operations . . . . The last thing we needed was for the CIA to be seized upon as something akin to a subverting influence in the affairs of other people. . . . We have grown up as a nation, respected for our free institutions and for our ability to maintain a free and open society. There is something about the way the CIA has been functioning that is casting a shadow over our historic position and I feel that we need to correct it." The U. S. government unconstitutionally withholds reporting to the public the total and major subtotals of annual Congressional appropriations for espionage, covert action, and other so-called intelligence activities. According to an estimate by the Associated Press, the total intelligence budget for fiscal

year 1997 is $30 billion, a highly excessive expenditure (57).

- The doctrine of "free trade," as reflected in the World Trade Organization and the North Atlantic Free Trade Agreement, is a permit to multinational organizations to exploit workers everywhere (58).
- The United States now conducts more than half of international arms trade. Over three–fourths of U. S. arms sales to the developing world in the past five years went to countries where citizens had no right to choose their own government, according to Ruth Leger Sivard (59).

2

SOVEREIGNTY

After citizens in town meetings have stated their principal political, social, and economic grievances – and little matter that they vary somewhat in pattern from place to place – their second step toward political remedy is to identify where sovereignty resides. To shed light on that identification, it is advisable first to review the two conceptualizations of the origin of sovereignty. One of them presumes present-day sovereignty was derived through a social contract from kings, and the other view sees sovereignty as a birthright.

THE SOCIAL CONTRACT

In the earliest of human times, before the founding of any governments, there was nowhere for sovereignty to reside except in individual human beings. Political philosophers such as Hobbes, Locke, and Rousseau in the seventeenth and eighteenth centuries visualized people in that ancient age living in "the state of nature." Those writers had different views of that nature. They agreed, however, that as time went on both the commonfolk and aristocrats felt insecure in person and property and addressed the problem by entering into some form of social contract. Individuals bargained away some self-determination of action in return for physical protection by the group. They thus delegated certain powers in mutually beneficial trade-offs. However, most individuals did not conceive of themselves as the sovereigns, did not have the foresight to arrange for retrieving powers misused, and thereby threw surrender of much sovereignty into the bargain. Individuals effectively did keep some sovereignty. Everywhere at all times, Professor M. Ginsberg states, "Power rests upon the will of the people in the sense that if stretched beyond a certain point, their acquiescence will not be secured, and social apathy and even disruption may result."

The early deals by individuals were made in every corner of the world with some monarch or oligarchy. A ruler whose authority began simply with the voluntary loyalty of a subject usually increased tremendously in power by formation of overwhelming military forces, alliances with religious institutions and various potentates, and acquisition of great wealth from taxation and conquest. That power, in many cases virtually absolute, was often claimed to be authorized by god, and – indistinguishable from sovereignty – held sway as "the divine right of kings" or something like it for thousands of years. Popular dissatisfactions arose from time to time, but effective moves by the people to recover their sovereignty have been very gradual. Early documents expressing the rights of man, such as Magna Charta and various subsequent English declarations of rights, were forthright assertions on certain aspects of liberty, but in effect were largely limited to diminishing the powers of the crown in favor of barons or parliament. Those were intermediate levels of government remote from the people.

Some present parliaments (including the British) assume that their powers were derived in this way from once-sovereign crowns, that the process legally conveyed sovereignty to them, and that consequently it is the parliaments which are the legitimate sovereigns. Yet there is a fatal flaw in this reasoning, namely, that no one, among the many who tried, ever convincingly demonstrated that any crown's claim to sovereignty was valid. Sanctification through divine grace satisfied the medieval mind, but such dogma surely has no standing in today's multi-religious and secular world. Fortunately, the social contracts between people in ancient times – no matter what their content or intent – cannot bind people down through the centuries to today.

BIRTHRIGHT SOVEREIGNTY

The simple valid alternative concept of the origin of sovereignty is this: Sovereignty, in equal measure, is the birthright of every person on earth, and that sovereignty is by nature untransferable. A sovereign may delegate certain powers to a government, but no democratic government has any sovereignty whatever. By reserving the word sovereignty to ultimate or original sovereignty and by using the word powers to mean temporary delegations of limited authority to representatives, it is possible to distinguish between these concepts and keep their relationships clear.

The first widely circulated writing to recognize inalienable ultimate sovereignty as a birthright apparently was *Two Treatises of Government* by John Locke in 1690. Even he did not use those terms, and evidently saw authority in civil society (popular sovereignty) rather than in individuals (personal sovereignty). Locke viewed humans beginning in "a state of perfect freedom . . . within the bounds of the law of Nature, without asking leave or depending upon the will of any other man." Then, he said, "The power that every individual gave the society when he entered into it can never revert to the individuals again, as long as the society lasts, but will always remain in the community; . . . so also when the society hath placed the legislative [power] in any assembly of men, with direction and authority for providing such successors, the legislature can never revert to the people whilst that government lasts." Locke relented on this dubious stricture, however, by adding, "But if they have set limits to the duration of their legislative, and made this supreme power in any person or assembly only temporary; or else when, by the miscarriage of those in authority, it is forfeited; upon the forfeiture of their rulers, or at the determination of the time set, it reverts to the society, and the people have a right to act as supreme."

WHERE SOVEREIGNTY RESIDES

There can be no doubt that sovereignty originally resided only in individuals. If sovereignty is untransferable (inalienable), as seems reasonable and just, any sovereignty that is in the hands of governments is improper transfer or usurpation. Governments may justly possess only temporary powers delegated to them by sovereign individuals.

Some functions of sovereignty are exercised by and as individuals

– personal sovereignty – and others by groups of sovereigns – popular sovereignty. The former is absolute authority, whereas the latter is a claim to authority which can be realized only when claimants have the will to organize as a nation and have the power to be independent of other nations.

Personal Sovereignty

It is difficult to trace historical development of the concept of sovereignty as a birthright. Following John Locke, those who came close to saying it during their discussions of sovereignty were Emmanuel Sieyes, Thomas Paine, James Wilson, James Madison, and George Mason. Thomas Jefferson believed that, "The God who gave us life gave us liberty at the same time." Perhaps the first person to state explicitly, in a widely circulated writing, that the individual is sovereign was John Stuart Mill in *On Liberty* in 1859.

Popular Sovereignty

The most unfortunate mistake in history has been the aforementioned common trade-off practice by individual sovereigns to protect their person and goods and to seek prosperity by surrendering sovereignty to some potentate or government. The constructive alternative, adopted ever more widely since the eighteenth century, has been for individual sovereigns to seek well-being by merging (not transferring) their personal sovereignty with other sovereigns to create composite popular sovereignty. This worthy trade-off can operate effectively only if a large proportion of the people within certain boundaries voluntarily agree to perform, or at least abide by the actions of others with respect to the six duties listed in the accompanying box.

DIFFERENT EXPERIENCES WITH SOVEREIGNTY

English Path to Sovereignty

In England, as late as the seventeenth century, sovereignty was still assumed to reside in the crown. This was so even though kings made concessions, mainly to the barons, through Magna Charta (1215) and acknowledged to their respective religious organiza-

Six Duties of Citizenship

- Become equal citizens of the specified nation.

- Keep sovereignty in the hands of the people and not transfer any of it to governments or any other organizations.

- Agree that collective sovereigns have the right to limit the rights of individual sovereigns only to keep one person from diminishing the sovereign rights of another person or, of secondary importance, to promote the public prosperity where feasible without adverse effect on personal liberty and justice.

- Delegate specific temporary powers to governments by means of a written constitution, which the people as popular sovereigns alone can legalize (ratify) and amend. This is constituent (constitution-building) sovereignty.

- Select representatives by universal voting (except youth, the mentally incompetent, and prisoners) to the governments created and instructed by the written constitutions. This is voting sovereignty.

- Agree to abide by laws derived from ratified constitutions and enacted by constitutionally elected legislators and executives.

tions that part of their claim to authority was by the grace of God. When the Commons in 1621 asserted their "ancient and indubitable birthright" to become involved in foreign affairs, religion, and state matters, King James I dissolved Parliament and, according to historian Samuel H. Beer, tore the offending pages from their journal. The hierarchic tradition, in which such events could take place, was a synthesis of classical and Christian thought. Among its notable synthesizers was Thomas Aquinas (1224-1274). "Both secular and ecclesiastical government enjoyed the consent of the governed," says Beer, "but it was the consent of deferment, not self-government." The Renaissance and Reformation were the beginnings of challenges to hierarchic authoritarian government, but changes in favor of the people came very slowly. Major contributors to the challenge included Machiavelli, Copernicus, Luther, Calvin, Knox, Montaigne, Bacon, and Galileo.

The Commons passed the Petition of Rights, condemning arbitrary taxation, imprisonment, and martial law, in 1628. Charles I reluctantly gave his assent, but during the following decade he and the lords substituted conciliar government for Parliament. Freedom of expression, recognition that deliberation by the many is superior to judgment by the few, and the view that citizens had a role in deciding on the common good were early advocated by John Milton in *Areopagitica* (1644). He visualized a sort of republic, but it was one governed by nobility and gentry and permitting suppression of books judged heretical or superstitious. In the following year or two were organized the Levellers, considered by some the first political party, who demanded that sovereignty be transferred to the House of Commons. They wanted manhood suffrage, true representation, decentralization, freedom of religion, and abolition of monopolies.

In the Commons at this time, representation was imposed from above by the king and was geographical. "It was only a short step from representating the whole people to deriving authority from them," in the judgment of historian Edmund S. Morgan. "By 1647," he added, "it was being argued that government officials, however appointed, gained their authority from the people." The belief that sovereignty was derived from the people was affirmed by Thomas Hobbes in *Leviathan* (1651), but he held that absolute power was irrevocably transferred to the king.

The desirability of a written constitution was early considered by John Lillburne and Richard Overton, leaders of the Levellers. They put forward a proposal called "The Agreement of the People." "What the Levellers sought," says Beer, "was a compact not among governments or communities but among individuals, stating the powers and limits of government at all levels." That document never became law. It was soon followed, however, by Oliver Cromwell's "The Instrument of Government," which was the first written constitution in the modern sense. It was operative only a few years.

The advantages of a written constitution were discussed by James Harrington in his *Oceana* (1656). The system of "orders" described there, according to Beer, was a "scheme of constitutional decentralization that foreshadows the federal structure adopted by the Americans." The royal restoration (Charles II and James II) put a damper on such movements. John Locke, previously observed as probably the first formally to espouse popular sovereignty, was in self-exile in Holland for five years before daring to return to England in 1688 and to publish his *Treatises of Government* in 1690. Similarly, Algernon Sidney wrote his *Discourses Concerning Government*, claiming the right of people to instruct their representatives and frequently change the form of government, in 1681-83 but did not publish it until 1698. Meanwhile, offer of the crown to William and Mary in 1689 was conditional on their concurring with the Declaration of Rights / Bill of Rights.

Locke, according to Professor William S. Carpenter, denied that sovereignty could exist anywhere except in the community as a whole and believed that the rights of individuals were inalienable. He further held that the people were superior to government, that limitations on government could be enforced only if embodied in a written constitution, and that powers delegated to governments were liable to forfeiture if the conditions of trust were not fulfilled. Legal scholar Sir William Blackstone in his *Commentaries* (1765-69) in England continued to accept the king as sovereign. A later eminent jurist, John Austin, during the 1830s advanced only enough to see the "King in Parliament" as the sovereign and thought power was safest in the hands of persons with appreciable property.

Despite discussion of the desirability of a written constitution, the British people (with a brief exception during Cromwell's time) never made actual moves toward one. They did, however, gradually reduce the power and role of the crown in favor of Parliament. During the 1770s, Green says King George III was still supreme. He not only directed ministers and troops and nominated judges

and bishops, but he also managed debates in Parliament and han-
dled all patronage. Then intermittently came a series of restraining
laws. Edmund Burke's Bill of Economical Reform in 1783 was "to a
great extent effectual in diminishing the influence of the Crown
over Parliament," says Green. During the 19th century Britain was
preoccupied with wars and empire building, but did increase the
powers of the House of Commons through notable reforms in
1832, 1867, and 1911.

American Path to Sovereignty

The first person in America to write about the people being sovereign was probably James Wilson (1742-1798) of Pennsylvania, a
signer of the Declaration of Independence and a member of the
Continental Congress, the Constitutional Convention, and the
convention's committee of detail responsible for preparing the draft
of the Constitution. As a scholarly lawyer, he concluded as early as
1770 that Parliament had no authority over the colonies. By the
middle 1770s he was espousing the sovereignty of the individual,
and during the convention he clearly stated that the proposed
national government was not "an assemblage of States, but of individuals for certain political purposes" (Malone). Thomas Paine in
Common Sense called for "a Constitution of our own."

Madison, Hamilton, and Jay, writing The Federalist papers in
1787-88, explained the new U. S. Constitution was framed "to promote such government on the basis of popular consent, not via
such delegated authority as might be grudgingly conceded by the
states." They added forthrightly that the ultimate authority
"resides in the people alone." James Wilson clarified the matter
further by stating, "As our constitutions are superior to our legislatures; so the people are superior to our constitutions." Historian
Morgan comments, "As the English House of Commons in the
1640s had invented a sovereign people to overcome a sovereign
king, Madison was inventing a sovereign American people to overcome sovereign states." Consistent with that, the U. S.
Constitution was ratified, not by the legislatures of the thirteen
states, but rather by delegates elected directly by the people to special conventions for that purpose.

French Path to Sovereignty

Political representation of the subjects of most European kingdoms and principalities from the later middle ages onward were in estates-general. The clergy made up the first estate, the nobility the second, and other privileged classes (mainly the town bourgeois) the third. Their discussions with the crown were usually only advisory. The French estates-general which assembled in 1614 did not meet again until 1789.

During the seventeenth century, largely under the rule of Louis XIV, according to the judgment of Francois Guizot, "the French government was at the head of European civilization; in the eighteenth century it disappeared; and it was French society, separated from its government, often opposed to it, that now preceded and guided the European world in its progress. . . . Perhaps there has never existed an absolute power more fully recognized by its age and nation, nor one which has rendered more real services to the civilization of its country and of Europe in general [than Louis XIV]. But by the very fact that this government had no other principle than absolute power, and reposed upon no other base than his, its decline became sudden and well merited." A feature of the eighteenth century, Guizot continued, was "the appearance of the human mind as the principal and almost the only actor. . . . [The change] began with ideas, with purely intellectual discussions, but it very soon terminated in events. The heads of intellectual parties soon became the heads of political parties. . . . I should be at a loss to say what external facts the human mind respected, or what external facts exercised any empire over it, but hated or despised the entire social state. It concluded, therefore, that it was called upon to reform all things; it came to consider itself a sort of creator; institutions, opinions, manners, society and man himself, all seemed to require reform, and human reason charged itself with the enterprise. What audacity equal to this had ever before been imagined by it!"

When the estates-general did resume meeting in 1789, the third estate, with nine-tenths of the population, became known as the Commons. Under the leadership of Abbe Emmanuel Sieyes, the Commons declared themselves the representatives of the nation and called themselves the National Assembly. Those from the clergy and

nobility could have a deliberative voice in it only if they forsook
membership in other estates and joined as national representatives.
The National Assembly claimed the constituent role and within three
weeks enacted the three foundation deeds of the Revolution – the
Declaration of the Rights of Man and of Citizens, the abolition of
feudalism, and introduction of the suspensive veto, allowing the king
to delay but not control acts of the National Assembly. The
Declaration states, "The nation is essentially the source of all sovereignty; nor can any individual, or any body of men, be entitled to any
authority which is not expressly derived from it." The nation, as the
term is used in France, means the French people and not the French
government, as Thomas Paine makes clear in his *Rights of Man*. He
states that the power of the French National Assembly originates in
the inherent right of the people. The Assembly completed its original
constituent role by enacting a constitution in 1791. Thereafter it pro-
ceeded to be the lower house of the French legislative body.

SOVEREIGNTY TODAY

In our time, U. S. Supreme Court Justice Owen J. Roberts spoke of
"the false doctrine of national sovereignty." He recognized only
"the sovereignty that abides in men, not in the state." Paddy
Ashdown, Liberal Democrats leader in the British Parliament, and
Philip Seguin, president of the French National Assembly, are others holding that view. Liberal Democrats, affirming their belief in
the sovereignty of the people, in 1990 issued a proposed written
constitution for the United Kingdom. A British organization,
Charter 88, was founded in 1988 advocating major structural
changes in the government. Two books (Hutton and Marr) support
the movement. Three-fourths of adult Britons think a written constitution is needed, according to a 1995 survey by Market &
Opinion Research International. Among the wanted provisions, as
reported by Barbash, are a bill of rights for individuals, freedom of
information, a referendum system, proportional representation,
decentralization, an elected upper house, independent judiciary, and
prohibition of special-interest gifts to members of Parliament.
Many want the decentralization to include home-rule legislatures

for Scotland, Wales, and Northern Ireland.

One responsibility of sovereigns is to decide to what extent they want to instruct representatives. Three centuries ago Harrington said, " 'Give us good men and they will make us good laws' is the maxim of a demagogue, and . . . exceedingly fallible. But 'give us good orders [constitutions], and they will make us good men' is the maxim of a legislator and the most infallible in politics." That still leaves open the question of how detailed a constitution should be and of how the electorate can otherwise guide a representative after election to office. Harrington recommended that any proposed bill should be debated for six weeks by letters and discourse between the people and representatives before enactment into law. He believed, says Beer, that "the representative is nothing else but an instrument or method whereby to receive the result [that is, the decision] of the whole nation."

When the late Senator Paul Douglas of Illinois was asked what guided him in casting votes, he replied that on a few issues he voted according to his personal conscience but that usually he tried to follow the wishes of his constituency. That seems like a satisfactory policy, partly because it leaves open the opportunity for citizen lobbying to be influential. Yet there is a third possibility that a minority – powerful because of money or position – might sway a representative's vote from either the majority or conscience. Whenever the people believe that their representatives are not pleasing them, they have the recourse of constitutional amendment – cumbersome as is the procedure – and should have available the quicker remedy of referendum. Electing a replacement is always a possibility, but that may be a long time off, and the new representative may or may not be more satisfactory.

An important sovereignty issue today is the challenge to the social contract by those wanting deregulation by government and the privatization of many activities traditionally managed publicly. Right after the industrial revolution, "The evils of a system which left the supply of basic economic wants to private industry insufficiently regulated by government became too flagrant to be overlooked," said Ernest A. J. Davies. Many public agencies, utilities, and programs followed, most of them appropriate. Those persons today who want to privatize such programs as retirement annuities, health care, home mortgages, schools, police, and parks are serving notice they want to withdraw from the historic social contract. They are confident in their own fitness – mentally, financially, and physically – to compete successfully in the unruly jungle or anarchy they seek. They confuse liberty with license, and have developed their sense of fairness no further than primitive survival of the fittest. Even in that rough arena, the privatizers will tolerate few impartial referees or umpires.

Privatization of public programs betrays the social contract when it arranges distribution of basic human services almost exclusively on ability to pay rather than on need or fair citizen shares. Privatization of fulfilling basic human needs, except when done by humanitarian organizations, also skims off undeserved profits, often arising from reduced quality and services. Claims by private enterprise to greater efficiency than public enterprise often can be demonstrated to be insupportable when, unlike biased business calculations, total benefits and total costs are compared. Real efficiency depends on good management, whether public or private, and only when performed openly and with responsible oversight.

One issue about sovereignty that is almost indeterminable is the valid size and boundaries of each civil society. It is related to the question of when is secession a right. The national government of the northern states of the United States did not allow the confederate states of the south to secede in 1861-65. Secessions have occurred in modern times when the Soviet Union and Yugoslavia broke up, and provinces such as Biafra and Quebec have come close to separation. One of the difficulties is that both a minority wanting secession and the majority, of which the minority is a part, have equal claims to sovereignty. When transnational federations begin to form, as discussed in Chapters 7 and 9, it will become more feasible for minority civil societies to secede from their nation while remaining a partner with that nation for specified purposes when both join a transnational federation.

Sovereign people exercise four powers, as diagrammed in Figure 1. Note that three different groupings – state, national, and transnational – are side by side and not one above the other in a hierarchy.

Figure 1

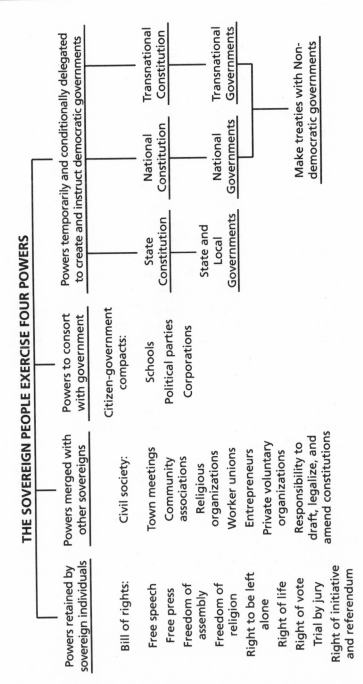

THE SOVEREIGN PEOPLE EXERCISE FOUR POWERS

Powers retained by sovereign individuals

Bill of rights:

Free speech
Free press
Freedom of assembly
Freedom of religion
Right to be left alone
Right of life
Right of vote
Trial by jury
Right of initiative and referendum

Powers merged with other sovereigns

Civil society:

Town meetings
Community associations
Religious organizations
Worker unions
Entrepreneurs
Private voluntary organizations
Responsibility to draft, legalize, and amend constitutions

Powers to consort with government

Citizen-government compacts:

Schools
Political parties
Corporations

Powers temporarily and conditionally delegated to create and instruct democratic governments

State Constitution

National Constitution

Transnational Constitution

State and Local Governments

National Governments

Transnational Governments

Make treaties with Non-democratic governments

3

THE PEOPLE ORGANIZE AND DIALOGUE

After the people state their problems and then reassure themselves that they as sovereigns are in charge, their third step toward a better society is to organize. They will have already organized town meetings to dialogue – a very important initial function. What logically would follow is the more complicated organization by the people for the purpose of performing their constituent (constitution-building) role.

History is full of occasions where the people have been pushed to be active enough to revolt, sometimes changing rulers. It is difficult to observe, however, where the people began to exercise self-government. One notable instance, reported by David Mathews, was at Dorchester, Massachusetts in 1633. Some cows had broken out of their yard and were grazing on the village green. John Maverick, a minister, reputedly said something to the effect, "We have a problem. We need to talk about it. Let's meet on Monday." That incident, says Mathews, created the first town meeting and established a political tradition which spread far and wide.

About that time in England, James Harrington sensed something rarely uttered – that the ordinary person has something to say about the common good which the elite does not know and can only learn from him. In the subsequent eighteenth century, Europeans like Walpole, Montesquieu, and Burke doubted the people's capability to exercise sovereignty. Yet Burke, conceding later that creation of the republican government in America proved his skepticism ill-founded, admitted "they have formed a new government sufficient for its purposes" and which "originated directly from the people."

INNOVATION AND ACTIVISM OF THE PEOPLE

Average townsfolk and rural people were basically involved in the founding of the United States. Competent and inspiring leaders played key roles, but the more enlightened saw themselves as part of a large public which was the main actor. That public, interestingly, proved to have more innovation and vitality than typical boards and bureaus of formal governments.

While the founding fathers of the United States were part of what some called a natural aristocracy, they did not consider themselves either an elite or delegates assigned to promote the special interests of their states. Rather they saw themselves more as part of the people, the novel concept historian Morgan says they invented. He believes that Madison as principal innovator "envisioned a genuine national government, resting for its authority, not on the state governments and not even on the peoples of the several states considered separately, but on an American people, a people who constituted a separate and superior entity, capable of conveying to a national government an authority that would necessarily impinge on the authority of the state governments."

"The first organizer of American democracy as a political force," believed Curtis Nettels, was Samuel Adams of Massachusetts in the 1770s. He was hostile to both the British government and the wealthy merchants of Boston. "To the management of the colony's affairs he proposed to bring the spirit of the New England town meeting," said Professor Nettels. "His first task was to free these plain people from their awe of their social and political superiors – to arouse among them a sense of their own importance. . . . His second task was to arouse the people to action. . . . In 1772 he induced the Boston town meeting to select a committee of correspondence to state the rights and grievances of the colonists, to communicate with other towns in the province, and to request them to draft replies."

Largely spontaneous committees of correspondence sprang up throughout the colonies. Meanwhile, where the royal governors dissolved the legal colonial assemblies or refused to call them to session, anti-British assembly members formed illegal assemblies. Additionally, there were town meetings and polls. These three kinds of informal groups, independent of any government, acted as the sovereign people and elected most of the delegates to the Continental Congress in 1774. It was not a meeting of governments, avers Andrew McLaughlin, but more like a political party convention. It "was founded not upon legally established governments but upon voluntary associations of individuals," observes Beer. He adds it was by no means all-inclusive in representation; yet "this movement was the 'constituent power' that created the new state."

Although the Continental Congress did not have a constitutional basis until the Articles of Confederation were ratified in 1781, that Congress did begin on November 3, 1775 authorization to the colonies to form state constitutions and governments. That is what Lincoln referred to when he said in his message to Congress on July 4, 1861, that, "The Union is older than any of the States, and, in fact, it created them as States."

Later important actions of the Continental Congress were to adopt a general resolution on May 10, 1776 making mandatory the creation of a republican government in each state, to proclaim the Declaration of Independence on July 4, 1776, and to call on February 21, 1787 for a constitutional convention. Members of the constitutional convention were chosen by state legislatures.

Ten provincial congresses (all but Massachusetts, Connecticut, and Rhode Island) during 1775-77 drafted constitutions, according to Nettels. "Since the congresses served at the same time as legislative bodies, there was little distinction between the constitution and ordinary law." Massachusetts led the way in 1799-80 toward more direct democracy. It called a special convention for framing its constitution and submitted the draft to a popular referendum.

FOUNDING FATHERS WERE INDEPENDENT, NOT JUST DELEGATES

It is worth noting here some of the ways in which the American founders were far more a part of the people composing an aborning nation than they were delegates of a state:

• When the Continental Congress wrote the Declaration of Independence in 1776, it referred eight times to "the people" as the concerned body and at no place to colonial, state, or local governments in that regard. When it introduced the term United States of America for purposes of declaration and action, it did so explicitly "by Authority of the good People of these Colonies" – not of the colonial governments. The point was emphasized by noting that "Legislative Powers . . . have returned to the People at large for their exercise."

- Although the members of the Constitutional Convention were appointed by the state legislatures and often kept in mind their local interests, they early disregarded the charge to have "the sole and express purpose of revising the Articles of Confederation." They dialogued less as delegates from a state than as individuals representing "We, the people of the United States." They used that phrase to specify – in the preamble to the Constitution – just who was ordaining it. Webster, during his debate with Hayne in 1830, analyzed that preamble as follows: "So far from saying that it is established by the governments of the several states, it does not even say that it is established by the people of the several states; but it pronounces that it is established by the people of the United States, in the aggregate. . . . It is in this, their collective capacity, it is as all the people of the United States, that they establish the Constitution."

- The convention draft of the constitution was sent to New York to the Continental Congress, which forwarded it to the states for ratification. It is significant to note that ratification was not by the state legislatures. The convention members specifically expressed the opinion that the constitution should "be submitted to a Convention of Delegates, chosen in each State by the People thereof" for ratification in order to become law.

THE PEOPLE OF THE U. S. IN THE 19TH AND 20TH CENTURIES

During the two centuries following establishment of the U. S. constitution and national government, the people practiced self-government in a variety of roles. They on occasion voted, served in office, lobbied, and – with regard to a practice unmentioned in the constitution – originated a multi-party political system. They fought a dreadful war to settle the issues of secession and slavery.

The people as constituent sovereigns, however, like Rip Van Winkle in Washington Irving's story, went to sleep for over two hundred years. Society and the world changed enormously during that time, but the people never formally proposed any constitutional amendments. There was considerable debate and popular movements regarding a few key issues – human rights, abolition of slavery, and widening of voter eligibility. Yet all twenty-six amendments made so far to the U. S. constitution were proposed by Congress. It is astonishing that the more significant of those amendments and various other possible amendments were not proposed directly by the people.

THE CONSTITUTION AND CIVIL SOCIETY TODAY

Article V of the constitution allows Congress to propose amendments or, on application of the state legislatures, to call a convention for proposing amendments. The constitution, however, does not say that only the Congress or state legislatures can propose amendments. Any constitutional provision which implied or said that would be an impermissible infringement of constituent sovereignty and thereby invalid. The people, without permission of their governments, are free to propose constitutional amendments and to organize constitutional conventions to legalize (ratify) them. The Tenth Amendment – unnecessarily stating the obvious and not adding a whit to its legitimacy – recognizes that powers not delegated to the national or state governments are reserved to the people. More accurate wording would have said, "reserved by the people." Surely, "the people" in special conventions (not the state legislatures) who legalized (ratified) the original constitution – and their descendants as well – have the sovereign right to propose and legalize amendments today, and to do so without any reference to governments other than to instruct them to set up polling facilities. Furthermore, it is the people – not Congress or state legislatures – which are the proper authority to specify how many voter signatures on a petition are a reasonable number to require for the calling of a constitutional convention.

It will be evident from any comprehensive set of grievances (such as illustrated in Chapter 1) that there is no likelihood that the U. S. Congress and state legislatures as now constituted would propose amendments for adequate constitutional reform. Thus the people must seize the initiative themselves. It will take both audacity and inventiveness. We can take heart from Justice Holmes, who observed "that the people – freely speaking and writing, freely listening, reading, and criticizing – are more likely to get at the truth of a matter than any other claimant to authority. The people are not infallible. . . . But the probabilities are on their side when they are compared with the old princes and prelates or the new presbyters and parliamentarians." (Beer)

As the people in town meetings expand their dialogue and actions to include constituent tasks, it is all the more important that they be as representative as possible. A help in this regard is to think in terms of the association in which they live, civil society. Civil society is the human relationships and space outside of government and the marketplace. Senator Bill Bradley says we make our homes, refine opinions, and bond our communities in civil society – "the sphere of our most basic humanity . . . [and] civilization."

How the People Organize Themselves

As civil society is so fundamental and additionally has the grave responsibility of writing constitutions to create and instruct governments, the question arises as to whether the actors in it – the people – are ready, or can become ready, to perform their tasks. A skeptic, Professor M. Ginsberg a half a century ago, believed, "The attempt to place sovereignty in the general will . . . must fail, since in this sense the general will is indeterminate and cannot therefore be vested in a person or persons." Ginsberg was unable to visualize how popular sovereignty can reside in individuals who organize to wield effective political action. As many today likewise say they can't quite picture it, there follows a description of some of the ways civil society is now organized and operates in the United States.

Of 186 million adults in the U. S. in the early 1990s, 160 million were actors in civil society as members of religious bodies, 96 million voted in the 1996 presidential election as a member of a party, some 100 million belonged to various citizen organizations (non-government and non-profit) initiated by the people, and 17 million were labor union members. Some organizational characteristics of each of the four groups are discussed in the following paragraphs.

(1) Many religious organizations are socially active in their communities. They sometimes are inspired to get into politics, even though often presenting themselves as independent individuals. Some religious leadership – notably the Catholic Church (including its liberation theology movement), Christian Coalition, and the Council of Churches – also are involved in state, national, and international politics. The effect of religion in politics is apparently increasing, according to two 1995 polls. One striking message of a U. S. News poll was that, "The country is divided largely by the fervency of religious belief." A Washington Post-Kaiser Foundation-Harvard poll, as reported by Thomas Edsall, found the electorate separated as to the deeply religious, moderately religious, and those not religious. The latter poll singled out Christian conservatives as "perhaps the fastest growing constituency in American politics."

The largest conservative interdenominational group in the U. S. is the Christian Coalition. It has 1.7 million members in 1,700 local chapters, is composed principally of evangelical Protestant Christians and conservative Roman Catholics, and is directed by Ralph Reed. It operates sophisticated grass-roots election campaigns for political offices from local school boards to president of the United States, according to Balz and Bernstein. Efforts of the Christian Coalition to impose their religious opinions on everyone through laws is considered improper by many. This led Norman Lear in opposition to organize People for the American Way, headed by Carole Shields. Before either of those groups, a progressive evangelical Sojourners Community was organized in urban Washington by Rev. Jim Wallis.

(2) Political parties were not viewed with favor by the founding fathers and were not mentioned in the Constitution. They are formed by the people in their civil society space, and the conventions they hold are not called by any government. Parties are "the makers of democratic government" and "form the principal institu-

tion for popular control of government," says William Keefe.

(3) About half of the membership of citizen organizations is in groups – like the American Association of Retired Persons, the American Automobile Association, and veterans organizations – where the leadership engages in political action and the rank-and-file usually confine their participation largely to dues paying and occasional letters to representatives or newspapers. An estimated one-sixth of members in civil society organizations are active participants in community and political affairs. These include parent-teacher associations, civil rights organizations, and women's groups. Membership in the remaining third of citizen organizations is ordinarily active, but it is more apt to be social, humanitarian, or professional than political. Typical of such organizations are the Red Cross, Salvation Army, Grange, Alcoholics Anonymous, amateur athletics, fraternal service groups, and occupational affiliations. One of the clear indications that the people are invigorating their civil society is the rise of new activist organizations insisting on change. They include 20/20 Vision, Working Group on Electoral Democracy, Concord Coalition, Share the Wealth, Corporation for National & Community Service, and Ashoka – Innovators for the Public.

(4) The 14 million union members were 35 percent of the U. S. labor force in 1945. However, the 17 million union members in 1995 were only 16 percent of the total. The implied decline of influence is partly the reason why the median wage declined 1 percent a year during 1989-93 while productivity rose 1.2 percent annually and corporation profits climbed even more. When John Sweeney became the new president of the AFL-CIO, he promised to transform the institution into a vibrant "social movement for economic justice," according to Steve Fraser and Nelson Lichtenstein. A major increase in organizing union membership is expected, especially among the underpaid. Women and minorities are gaining larger roles in unions. As the influence of labor is restored, one may expect more equal bargaining with management, less employer coercion and intimidation, enforcement of workplace health and safety laws, and shorter work weeks. An organization called Working Today, enrolling individual citizens rather than

employee groups, is being formed to support labor, reports David Warsh.

The churchgoing, voting, organizational, and union activities mentioned above demonstrate that civil society in America is indeed very active. The decline of interest in bowling leagues and various other community activities led Robert Putnam to see it in 1994 as decay. A little later, however, Wray Herbert noticed signs of a renaissance in American public life. These included a three-day community forum in Waterville, Maine, to guide future education and prosperity measures; a project in Tylerville, Texas, to train community leaders; a group in Chattanooga, Tenn., called A DARE to Parents which challenged adults to reexamine their own lives and then neighborhood problems; a partnership between activists and business in Cleveland, Ohio's West Side neighborhood to create and upgrade jobs; and citizen organizations, supported by the Pew Charitable Trust and local church leaders, in the Frankford section of Philadelphia, to help entrepreneurs, a basketball league, and police recruitment. Herbert mentions sociologist Harry Boyte's belief that participating in public works creates a strong sense of citizenship. Further, he quotes political scientist Benjamin Barber, "Americans are homeless. They're longing for a civic home. And they know it's not Washington, and it's not the mall."

"Failure to appreciate the importance of civil society lies at the core of our policy dilemma," again quoting Senator Bill Bradley. It is the place, he adds, "where we live our lives, educate our kids, worship our God, and associate with our neighbors." Bradley, along with Jeremy Rifkin and Peter Drucker, see civil society as a major site of future jobs. They believe the businesses and governments which are reducing employment should allocate part of their resources to creating paid community jobs. Community workers are apt to be more service-oriented than average and to be helping to solve our most pressing social problems. "Within civil society," continues Bradley, "lies the zest to deal with what ails us as a nation." A perceptive and inspiring guide of how people can come together in "public life" to improve their lives and their communities is The *Quickening of America* by Frances Moore Lappe and Paul Martin Dubois.

It is astonishing how widespread is the erroneous assumption that progress and prosperity are dependent on the crutch of generating economic booms. There are two major flaws in the conception of the desirability of promoting greater economic growth per capita in industrialized countries. One result is that expanded production is less efficient than a stable economy because the costs in environmental degradation are greater than the sum of the benefits. The fault with economic-growth promotion, as pointed out by Robert Theobald, is that it detracts attention and resources from the far more important prescription for progress and prosperity – "building social cohesion." Useful critiques of the concept of growth have been written by Daly and Douthwaite.

The next question that arises is whether present social, religious, political, and other citizen organizations and activities are sufficient grounds for believing that the people may be ready and capable for the great leap to reform our Constitution.

A first condition is evident – the people are discontent with their government. The fact that 51 percent of eligible voters did not participate in the 1996 presidential election may have been due less to indifference than to the well-grounded belief that none of the candidates would represent them very well. Some may have been astute enough to realize that until procedures and policies were changed, it would not matter much which individuals sat in the official chairs.

"Most elected officials don't care what people like me think." That view was expressed by eight out of ten people surveyed in 1994 by the Times Mirror Center for the People & the Press. Similarly, Arthur Levine's 1993 survey of 9,100 college students showed that only 21 percent believed "Congress has the interests of the people at heart." Over half thought "meaningful social change cannot be achieved through traditional American politics." More than half of the Times Mirror respondents thought the U. S. should have a third party.

Now let us ask ourselves if the people are widely disenchanted with their government, does a substantial majority of them have political philosophies receptive to altering the Constitution. Two surveys of such philosophies suggest maybe so. The 1994 Times Mirror survey divides Americans into ten groups and estimates the percentage of each in the total U. S. population. If all those the survey classified as partisan poor, new dealers, seculars, embittered, and new economy independents were combined with most of the new Democrats and bystanders, they would add up to two-thirds of the total. The one-third assumed to be opposed to constitutional reform and thus left out would be the so-called enterprisers, most of the moralists, and half of the libertarians.

Another political survey was conducted in 1995 by U. S. News. It subdivided U. S. adults into seven categories and estimated the portion of each in the national total. If one combined all those classified as populist traditionalists with most of the so-called liberal activists, ethnic conservatives, and agnostics and with a minority of the conservative activists, stewards, and dowagers, they again would add up to two-thirds of the total. The third left out, as not expected to be reformers, are a majority of the conservative activists, stewards (business-oriented), and dowagers and a minority of other groups.

EXTENSIVE DIALOGUE TO PRECEDE DECISION-MAKING

The central process of popular government is rational deliberation, as some as early as Milton recognized. Government by discussion was institutionalized in parliament, says Beer, and accorded major importance by Hume. As regards founding of the United States of America, James Wilson viewed individual reflection and collective deliberation as the heart of the process, says Beer. Accordingly, there were four months of discussion in the Constitutional Convention and a notable nine-month public dialogue, based largely on The Federalist papers by Hamilton, Madison, and Jay, prior to the vote where the people decided whether or not to accept the Constitution draft.

At the outset and during all dialogue there should be available pertinent facts and all sides of opinion as to the issues discussed. The results of polls and referendums are seldom useful when they are instantaneous, spontaneous, and off-the-cuff. Two New Hampshire candidates for the U. S. House of Representatives, as reported by Hank Nichols in 1994, have told citizens they, if elected, would cast their votes in Congress according to opinions called into them on toll-free lines. Two-thirds of those polled by the

American Talk Issues Foundation favor Congress' establishing an office of public opinion research and arranging binding national referendums on major issues, according to Kevin Merida and David S. Broder. Having little regard for quick polls before extended dialogue, secretary of health, education, and welfare David Mathews in the Ford administration, made the pertinent observation that, "Greater popularization is not necessarily greater democratization. . . . A collective knee-jerk is no better than an individual knee-jerk."

As a case in point, The Center for International and Security Studies, University of Maryland, reported that the mean estimates by persons polled as to the share of U. S. military budget going to U. N. peacekeeping was 15 percent and that that was considered too much. When told the actual amount was 1 percent, respondent disapproval of the U. S. contribution dropped from 58 to 18 percent.

"The crucial ingredient that distinguishes a mass of people from a responsible public is the opportunity for deliberation, time to absorb information and exchange views," says David Broder. A "Civic Declaration" by the National Center for Neighborhood Enterprise, Harry Boyte of the University of Minnesota, Benjamin Barber of Rutgers, et al. in 1994 urged citizens to expand greatly their community deliberation, reported E. J. Dionne Jr. Useful, objective, and comprehensive discussion papers on a wide variety of public issues are prepared by the League of Women Voters, the Kettering Foundation (headed by David Mathews at Dayton, Ohio), Foreign Policy Institute, and some other organizations. Daniel Yankelovich, public opinion analyst, points out ways to improve public judgment and enable that judgment to influence specialists and political leaders so as to result in better policies.

In the best of dialogues, participants are face-to-face, together long enough to become somewhat acquainted, and are representative of the community to which they belong. It is logistically impossible for the people of a nation to organize themselves in a way to meet those standards perfectly. However, approximations can be arranged which are reasonably satisfactory. It is instructive to recognize that every existing government, including that of the United States, was conceived and ordained by procedures unable to involve much of the population.

The most suitable forum for political dialogue is the town meeting. This "town" may be an actual small town, a part of a city – block, precinct, ward, cluster, quarter, zone, district, neighborhood, or community – or scattered individuals from a rural or large area who assemble. A town meeting is ordinarily called by by a civic association, a local government, or some non-partisan citizen organization with no special interest. It is always open to the public and welcomes participation by anyone. Such a town meeting meets the desired characteristic of being face-to-face, and in addition the participants often know each other in varying degrees. There is no assurance how representative the participants are, as they appear voluntarily.

The matter of representation leads David Irwin, from Peterborough, New Hampshire, to be a might skeptical when the media treats the town meeting as "unsullied democracy." He has seen them limited by the size of town halls and by the absence of elderly who find hard chairs uncomfortable, young parents who can't afford baby sitters, and the apathetic. He sees their places overrepresented by attendees with special interests in schools, sports, and various other services. As New Hampshire legislators seemed to believe that voters favoring lower taxes outnumber those wanting more public services, they passed legislation allowing secret ballots in place of town meetings. Yet even if decision-making voting is reduced or eliminated in town meetings, it would be worthwhile to preserve and expand the process for the great value of the dialogue aspect alone.

So, to return to the main theme of this book, it would be well if as many citizens as possible worldwide would get together in communities and have town meetings. There for, say, a year voluntary participants could discuss what kind of government they want and what they would like it to do. "Big decisions about economic policy and government activity should not be left to experts," says former budget chief Alice Rivlin. She adds, "Unless substantial numbers of citizens make the effort to get into the discussion – to think and talk and argue about what kind of economy they want and what they and their elected leaders should do – the country will not function well." To help the process along, the League of Women Voters is establishing a Center for Community Dialogue offering "training in facilitation, consensus building, collaborative decision-making, and conflict management."

The increasing participation of religious organizations in politics raises the question of what role is appropriate for them in town meetings. Religious institutions, like any other group with ideas and programs, have every right to inspire or appoint delegates to speak for their institution or themselves. Hopefully religious doctrines – like salvation, conceptions of deities, and designations of what is scripture – which vary greatly from one denomination to another – will always be recognized as outside the sphere of general civic dialogue. Many valid political questions, however, have a bearing in some people's minds to doctrine and may be usefully addressed by focusing discussion on the pertinent root issues. For example, before any legislation is enacted on, say, birth control, abortion, sexual orientation, and living styles of unmarried couples, town meetings should dialogue on when moral principles should be left to individual decisions – out of bounds to government action – and when, as in the cases of stealing or arson, they are prohibited by law. As another example, town meetings would do well to avoid discussion of the pertinence of prayer and revelation and instead deal with the root matter of in what manner and where they are appropriate – home, religious institution, school, or elsewhere.

When public dialogue gets into religious and ethical issues, a virtue apt to suffer is tolerance. Officials of the Christian Coalition, fundamentalist churches, and certain other religious and secular organizations are generally viewed as prejudiced against women's equal rights, scholarly history, science, and gay lifestyles. Director Reed of the Christian Coalition, according Balz and Bernstein, "has gone out of his way to portray his movement as sympathetic to other religions and open-minded on issues of race and tolerance." He believes this has helped bring his organization to, "A place at the table, a sense of legitimacy and a voice in the conversation that we call democracy." If Reed can persuade his followers to lean toward that high ground, perhaps members of all traditional and legendary religions can dialogue with those of natural and unfolding religions to meet in the middle ground of family values and humanitarianism. One move in this direction is the Millennium Moment Initiative, led by Gerald O. Barney, formerly director of "The Global 2000 Report to the President," in collaboration with the Council for a Parliament of the World's Religions. The Initiative is designing "suitable 'rites of passage' through which people will 'die' to old 20th century ways of thinking and being, and emerge as new 21st century people [working toward] a sustainable future." It is "building leadership commitments in Christianity, Islam, Judaism, Hinduism, Buddhism, Baha'i, Shinto, Indigenous, and other faith traditions to making the year 2000 a turning point." Various community and national meetings are programmed for the next few years and a global conference in Iceland in 2000.

It is difficult to predict how much of the population, even in countries accustomed to democracy, might participate in town meetings considering constitutional reform. Even if a supportive movement snowballs, the turnout is apt to be insufficiently representative. There are, however, supplemental ways appreciably to publicize the dialogue. Granada Television in Britain during election years since 1974 has arranged for some 500 voters to meet for two weeks of discussion and then to question political leaders on a telecast program titled Granada 500. The participants were from several localities selected as statistically appropriate microcosms of the whole country and which made getting together convenient. The program has been sufficiently popular so that many viewers, although not participating in the meetings, heard the presentation of facts and opinions and observed the effects of discussion.

Similar "deliberative opinion polls" or "national caucuses" can "provide the possibility of recreating the conditions of the face-to-face society in a manner that serves democracy in the large-scale nation-state," says government professor James S. Fishkin, University of Texas. He inspired assembly of 459 representative citizens, selected by professional polling techniques, in a National Issues Convention at Austin, Texas, in January 1996. For a weekend they dialogued with each other in small groups, with experts, and with presidential candidates on family, economic, and international issues. The Public Broadcasting Service (PBS) televised some of the dialogue and of the results of participant polls, with emphasis on the degree to which opinions changed as a result of the dialogue. Such programming largely avoids media and party dominance and filtering of the presentation. Electronic town halls proposed by Robert A. Dahl, Amitai Etzioni, and others can reach even wider audiences and additionally allow the important feature of talk-back.

It is well to recognize that many people say they not only don't have time to attend a town meeting but not even to stay home and watch one televised either. A suggestion to such people is that they find extra time by shortening to some extent the hours spent on entertainment programs of TV and radio, the frivolous parts of newspapers, and the overconsumption aspects of shopping.

4

DECLARATION OF SOVEREIGNTY, RIGHTS, AND RESPONSIBILITIES

After the people have adequately dialogued about their grievances, sovereignty, and organization, the fourth recommended topic is to discuss the social contract they have with each other. Following extended discussion at town meetings and elsewhere, the people can make written declarations affirming their sovereignty, specifying their birthrights, and acknowledging their responsibilities to one another. There is no need for each person and community to arrive at a declaration with identical wording. Likewise one cannot expect the reaching of unanimity on specifics. However, part of the exercise should be to develop declarations that approximate consensus. The social contract, it should be kept in mind, is something that is recognized before any action to form or modify a government and is only tangentially related to government.

This concept was well expressed by historian John E. Selby, professor at the College of William and Mary, as follows: "American thinking slowly evolved toward a distinction between the sovereignty of the people and the authority of even the most popularly elected branch of government. Contemporary political theorists often explained this distinction by invoking the concept of a social covenant through which the people established a society with guarantees of individual freedom before entering a separate political compact with a ruler or rulers to govern according to these dictates."

Thus it is more appropriate for a bill of rights to be in a separate document as part of the social contract, than to be a part of a constitution. The first American bill, Virginia's Declaration of Rights (1776), by some combination of intent and oversight, was not included in the state's original constitution. The founding fathers of the United States did not think it necessary to include a bill of rights in the original constitution. They apparently believed such personal rights were outside the jurisdiction of the government which was being built. It may be reasoned that such rights are inherent rights whose validity is not increased by inclusion in a constitution. Madison changed his mind and proposed such a bill as the first ten amendments. The reasons for his second thoughts apparently were to gain from George Mason and Patrick Henry support for the constitution and to specify which rights the national government could not infringe. Later the 14th amendment cited rights the state governments could not infringe. Both stipulations were clarifying, but they were negatives. It would be useful to express human rights in a positive way. Historic documents contributing to evolution of the concept include Magna Charta (1215), English Declaration / Bill of Rights (1689), Virginia Declaration of Rights (1776), French Declaration of the Rights of Man (1789), United States Bill of Rights (1791), and the United Nations Declaration of Human Rights (1948). The latter was prepared by a commission chaired by Eleanor Roosevelt. Although the U N document is not a treaty enforceable by law, it is a widely respected standard that has influenced many treaties, constitutions, and declarations.

A lot less attention has been accorded to responsibilities corresponding to rights. Thomas Paine reported that some members of the French National Assembly thought that its Declaration of Rights should be accompanied by a Declaration of Duties. Paine, believing the additional language unnecessary because the duties were obvious, said, "A Declaration of Rights is, by reciprocity, a Declaration of Duties also. Whatever is my right as a man, is also the right of another; and it becomes my duty to guarantee, as well as to possess." Contemporaneously, Amitai Etzioni, as reported by Warren Ross, believes "strong rights presumes strong responsibilities" but sees "a painful imbalance between our readiness to claim rights and our unwillingness to shoulder responsibilities." Ross also presents a ten-point bill of responsibilities proposed by John F. Smith III.

It would be instructive for each person to draft a Declaration of Sovereignty, Rights, and Responsibilities composed by themselves and then discuss them at town meetings and constitution conventions. Declarations could be something like the following:

Declaration of Sovereignty, Rights, and Responsibilities

I affirm that I am a sovereign, all other individuals are likewise sovereign, and no government or association has any just sovereignty. I affirm the right voluntarily to merge personal sovereignty with others to become part of a composite popular sovereignty.

My liberty includes freedom of life, conscience, thought, speech, religion, writing, printing, peaceful assembly, privacy, travel, and self-control of my mind and body, including reproductive choice, medical treatment, terminal illness, sexual preference, and use of drugs not harmful to others. No power is delegated to any government to abridge these rights.

Other inalienable rights of mine are a birth certificate with names of natural parents, a national passport, and – if charged with a crime – a speedy public trial by jury. The appropriate branch of government is ordered to provide such documents and trials without formulating any conditions which abridge these rights. Fairness and equal opportunity in elections are always to be considered sufficiently superior in principle to permit substantial limitations on expenditures in election, initiative, or referendum political campaigns.

As a constituent sovereign, I order the government of each state, whenever five percent of eligible voters shall so request by signing a specific petition, to place on the ballot of the next regular election, proposed constitutional amendments or candidates for representation at a constitutional convention.

As a balance to my claimed rights, I accept the responsibility to help guard the liberties of others, to care about other people including those with different beliefs, to vote, to serve on juries, to return at least as much to society as I benefit from it, to be a steward of the earth, and to live by a system of democratic laws. Those responsibilities are inherent in the process of merging personal sovereignty into popular sovereignty, writing democratic constitutions, and establishing representative just governments.

I pledge to do my utmost to help organize periodic neighborhood town meetings, to try to participate in them about monthly, and to serve actively on one or more of their committees.

Part II

THE PEOPLE REFORM CONSTITUTIONS

5

POWERS TO THE PEOPLE AND
REMOVED FROM CORPORATIONS

After the people make the fundamental move of setting up periodic town meetings, their primary goal should be to reinstruct their governments by means of reformed constitutions.

AMENDING CONSTITUTIONS

The principal vehicle for putting into effect the proposals made here is the constitutional amendment. Some, with little thought, view a constitution as a totem very seldom if ever to be altered. They say, off the cuff, don't open up the constitution to tampering or you are likely to end up with something worse. That shows little faith in democracy and even less recognition of how much of today's situation is appreciably worse than the founding fathers ever could foresee.

Thomas Jefferson, late in life, expressed the view that the creators of the U. S. constitution did a tolerably good job, but that each generation should revise it to suit the changed circumstances of their time.

Representative George McDuffie of South Carolina observed in 1824: "It has often been urged in conversation that, by making amendments of the Constitution, we should impair the popular veneration for that instrument. . . . Nothing can be more dangerous than the inculcation of this sort of superstitious idolatry in this country. Its inevitable tendency is to confound the vices of our system with the system itself; and, in that way to convert the best feelings of the community into the means of preventing the correcting of imperfections which time must disclose in all human institutions, and of perpetuating abuses from which no government administered by men has ever been exempted." (Hyneman and Carey).

Some of those unenthusiastic about amending constitutions are also extremist in wanting to keep constitutions general and short. This, of course, leaves it to courts, legislators, and presidents – a step removed from the people – to make interpretations, often little different from amendments. Nevertheless, one of the remarkable aspects of the U. S. Constitution is its brevity. That worthy objective, encompassing the minimum of legal jargon, however, resulted in inclusion of many generalizations, especially as regards to policy. If subsequent officeholders had been extraordinarily wise and noble, such generalizations may have sufficed. History has shown they were not, particularly in their tendency to serve power structures rather than the people as a whole. Experience has demonstrated that the sovereign people cannot be well served until they provide officeholders much more explicit instructions than are contained in existing constitutions.

When people do set up the periodic town meetings aimed at constitutional reform, it would be proper for the first subject on the agenda to be relocation of power – political, social, and economic. Top priority within that context should be to identify those powers of personal sovereignty and of popular sovereignty (discussed in Chapter 2) which the sovereigns wish to keep to themselves, to take back in cases where they have been usurped, and jealously to avoid delegating to any government. Those powers should be placed in a Declaration of Sovereignty, Rights, and Responsibilities (Chapter 4).

DIRECT DEMOCRACY

The second priority in discussing relocation of power would be for the people to recognize some of the limitations of representative government and to provide occasions whereby sovereign citizens directly initiate proposed laws – without reference to legislatures or executives – and decide by popular vote whether to approve them as laws. Similar referendums could be used by the people to test their approval of laws passed by legislatures. Such laws as approved by referendum – whether initiated by the people or a legislature – would become amendments to existing law and would not be subject to veto. This is direct democracy.

The citizen initiative and referendum system has been used in Switzerland often since the 1860s. Father Robert Haire of South Dakota and publisher Benjamin Urner of New Jersey in 1885 made the first such proposal for the United States national government, according to David Schmidt. Oregonians in 1906 were the first petition signers in the United States to get an initiative by the people on a state ballot. Supporters of the referendum system have included Samuel Gompers, Eugene Debs, William Jennings Bryan, Hiram Johnson, Theodore Roosevelt, Woodrow Wilson, Jerry Brown, Senator Alan Cranston, Senator James Abourezk, Ralph Nader, Barry Commoner, Jack Kemp, Senator Mike Gravel, and Pat Choate. Twenty-three states (including seventeen west of the Mississippi River) have adopted procedures for using the initiative and referendum system in state matters. The people's right to initiative and referendum should be part of a bill of rights (Chapter 4) and also to be recognized in the national constitution so as to apply to all citizens and without needing the consent of state governments. The principal conditions for prudent exercise of initiative and referendum, according to Schmidt, are media access, voter information, and a petition requirement high enough to prevent ballot clutter and low enough to enable grassroot groups to qualify an initiative for the ballot.

With regard to national issues, even if the U. S. Congress were willing to share its lawmaking function with the people voting in a referendum, any Congressional move in that direction would be unconstitutional because the constitution authorizes only the Congress to make national laws. So if the American people want the right to have national referendums, on any subject other than the already-specified right to ratify proposed amendments, they must so amend the Constitution. The initial question to be dealt with is who has the right of initiative, i.e. the right to propose the pertinent amendment, to propose a proposition to be voted on in a referendum, and to specify the conditions (e.g. number of petition signatures required) for a proposition to qualify for a place on the ballot. We previously noted that just because the Constitution states that Congress may propose amendments and because that is the only way amendments have been initiated to date, it does not mean there is not another way to propose amendments. Surely the people, as civil society, can organize a procedure, even if it takes innovation, for their proposing amendments, just as members of political parties organize political conventions without any reference to the Constitution or to national or state governments.

BRIDLING BIG BUSINESS CORPORATIONS

The third priority at town meetings in discussing relocation of power would have to do with reducing and democratizing the runaway power of big business corporations. That power has become so mighty than until it is leashed, there will be no possibility of any appreciable reform to solve the major problems of our society. To put the matter bluntly and succinctly, the most fundamental political, social, and economic problem in democracies today is that big business corporations have too much power, exercise much of it unethically to control government and other parts of our lives, and are insufficiently regulated by the democratic process. This intolerable situation is detailed particularly well in recent books by Charles A. Reich, David Korten, Kevin Phillips, Charles Lewis, Michael Lind, Richard J. Barnet, and Ralph Estes.

Only a system that reallocates political responsibilities subnationally and transnationally "can combine the power required to rival global market forces with the differentiation required of a public life that has hopes to inspire the reflective allegiances of its citizens," says political scientist Michael Sandel. We need a change that "reorients power relationships," says Senator Bill Bradley. He makes clear he doesn't want to stigmatize success, but calls for a private sector which flourishes "in a way more responsive to national purpose." Then he says precisely what should change – money from corporations and others corrupting the political system, employee job insecurity, unfair profit sharing, business transferring its private environmental costs to citizens, neglect of the long run to maximize short-term gain, and incomplete reporting of activities.

The misbehavior of business corporations is well analyzed by Estes, particularly as regards their departures from the original intent of serving the public and their neglect of stakeholders other than stockholders, viz., workers, consumers, and communities. He would like managers to issue a much more comprehensive "scorecard" of their corporation's activities. If the managers performance were measured against such broad criteria rather than just the bottom line of shareholder profits, Estes believes corporations would act more responsibly. He prefers that this be done voluntarily, but is willing to suggest a Corporate Accountability Act as a last resort. Estes' scorecard for the public would include transparency about company ownership, taxes paid, and lobbying; past actions and future plans for employee layoffs, plant closings, and pension funds; records of claims of injury from products, violations of government regulations, and employee grievances; identification of materials used and wastes discharged; and the corporation's impact on schools, water, traffic, and the environment. Making such information readily available would undoubtedly be helpful to workers, consumers, and communities in bargaining with corporations. Yet that alone, even if mandatory, would not be apt to go very far in reforming corporations.

Those parts of big business policy which are the most irresponsible and most damaging to individuals and society are usually implemented through corporate influence on government. So the most pressing need is to staunch the enormous flow of money and favors from corporations into the hands of candidates and government officeholders. Much of that money is spent for expensive and sophisticated campaign strategies, for dominating candidate exposure in the television, radio, and newspaper media, and for heavy mailings, telephone calls, and home visits. It assures that most of those elected will be either persons handpicked by business corporation agents or persons for other reasons deeply committed to supporting special privileges for big business in our society. James Raskin and John Bonifaz view this situation as a barrier to political participation. They call the initial kind of such elections a "wealth primary" because candidates have no chance of winning unless they can raise huge sums of money first, according to E. J. Dionne, Jr. As a result, "We don't have representative government," says Fred Wertheimer, former president of Common Cause. "The American public believes that Congress no longer represents them," adds Joan Claybrook, president of Public Citizen.

After repeated shilly-shallying by Congresses and Presidents failed to address the issue, editors of the *Washington Post* in 1995 denounced, "The fetid system by which the country finances political campaigns." Wertheimer had warned, "The credibility of Congress cannot be restored as long as the corrupt campaign finance system continues. The deep cynicism that is doing so much harm to the health of our political system cannot be overcome until fundamental reform occurs." "Campaign finance reform is essential," added E. J. Dionne, Jr., "if we're to preserve not just the form but also the substance of democracy."

STOPPING CORPORATE CONTROL OF GOVERNMENT IS UNCONSTITUTIONAL

It is very unlikely that the Congress either would or could effectively reform campaign financing. A basic obstacle is that in 1886 the U. S. Supreme Court, in *Santa Clara County v. Southern Pacific Railroad*, ruled that business corporations are "persons" entitled as much as any other person to equal protection of the laws as specified in the Fourteenth Amendment. Then in 1976 in *Buckley v. Valeo*, the Supreme Court, looking at the Federal Election Campaign Act of 1971 as amended in 1974, upheld government rights to limit the contributions of individuals directly to a candidate but invalidated all other restrictions on campaign expenditures as violation of the First Amendment. This meant that federal or state legislatures could not put any ceiling on the amount of money spent on political campaigns as long as the channeling was indirect, such as through a political party (often called "soft money").

The issue surfaced again in 1978, when in *First National Bank of Boston v. Belloti* the Supreme Court held that corporation rights to First Amendment protection included political speech. In that case, it ruled that the state of Massachusetts could not prohibit corporations from spending money on a ballot referendum. In 1990, however, in *Austin v. Michigan State Chamber of Commerce*, the Court allowed Michigan to limit corporate speech (including spending) to counteract "the corrosive and distorting effects" of "corporate wealth," according to Ruth Marcus. Furthermore, the

Court recognized that the wealth of any corporation was accumulated partly from persons not sharing the corporation's political posture and therefore upheld prohibiting corporations from making political expenditures except those voluntary contributions to a corporation's political action committee. Regarding this case, Justice Thurgood Marshall took the position that the fairness of political debate was a more compelling state interest than placing no restrictions on free speech. "Expression that is itself destructive of the political process is self-defeating in terms of the purpose of the First Amendment," commented University of Chicago law professor Geoffrey Stone. He added that "corporate speech in certain circumstances can overwhelm the political process."

CORPORATE WRONGDOING

Crime

Corporations are a social and economic problem mainly by exercising their enormous power and wealth to corrupt government, but also as a result of criminal tendencies. The Manville Corp., A. H. Robbins Co., and Philip Morris manufactured products (namely asbestos products, Dalkon Shield contraceptives, and cigarettes, respectively) which investigations indicated caused major health injuries. Furthermore, critics reported that they withheld from consumers the results of scientific tests on the products and circulated misleading advertising about them. Reebok makers of athletic shoes, regional bottlers of Coca Cola and Pepsi Cola, and food giant Archer Daniels Midland Co. are among firms which have paid millions of dollars in fines for price fixing. GNP Commodities, Inc. was fined $1 million for allowing customers to be cheated in the Chicago Mercantile Exchange, and Michael R. Milken, the "junk bond king," of Drexel Burnham Lambert, Inc. pleaded guilty to rigging stock prices and stealing money and agreed to pay $600 million in penalties, according to the Wall Street Journal. Bell Helicopter Textron returned $90 million to the U. S. government to resolve allegations it fraudulently overcharged the Army for spare parts. The Federal government loses more than $400 million a year in royalties because certain oil companies underreport their

withdrawals from public lands. Mislabeling of octane rating at gaso-
line pumps has been cheating motorists, who are delivered regular
grade and paying for premium grades, $150 to 600 million a year,
says the General Accounting Office.

Unearned Income
Much of the unearned income by corporations is not viewed by its
owners as stealing because it is legal. Such legal arrangements
rammed through Congress by corporate power, comprise a wide
variety of "incentives" in the form of tax concessions and subsidies.
These are estimated to cost $90 billion a year, according to Robert
J. Shapiro, Progressive Policy Institute. Among the most outra-
geous are the very small fees paid by agribusiness corporations for
huge quantities of public water, by ranchers for grazing on public
lands, by timber corporations for cutting trees in public forests, and
by mining companies for extracting minerals from public lands.
Federal grazing fees are about one-fifth of those paid to owners of
private land. When a firm obtained a mining claim that may yield
$10 billion worth of gold, with a return to the U. S. Treasury of
$10,000, Interior Secretary Bruce Babbitt called it "the biggest gold
heist since the days of Butch Cassidy." Of course a bigger heist is
the some $80 billion which Savings and Loan businessmen lost and
have pinned on the citizenry. "The American government has
become a machine for the conversion of public assets into private
profits, and a big machine for the conversion of private liabilities
into public liabilities," says Arjun Makhijana, Institute for Energy
and Environment Research. An example of the latter is the commitment of the U. S. Federal government to accept from electric
companies the high-level radioactive waste from commercial
nuclear reactors even though a half century of research has failed to
develop an acceptable technology for safe storage.

Subversion and Hucksterism
Yet another perverse kind of activity – technically legal but ethically
criminal – was when Del Monte and the International Telephone
and Telegraph Co., respectively, encouraged the Central
Intelligence Agency to overthrow the democratically elected

governments of Arbenz in Guatemala in 1954 and of Allende in Chile in 1973 in order to favor their business pursuits. More recently, since the CIA is no longer occupied with Soviet tyranny, corporations are trying to get the agency to devote much of its efforts to stealing and supplying them with commercial secrets. On the vulgar and tawdry side, holidays meant to honor our patriots and religions are demeaned by the hucksters who hawk Washington birthday sales, Memorial Day sales, and Easter sales. Other blatant merchants cheapen and interrupt sporting events by excessive incessant plastering of their names and trademarks on surfaces where television cameras are trained and in captions defacing the viewing screens. Many landscapes, historical sites, and roads are made ugly by commercial billboards. Sponsors not permitted to place their offensive signs close to highways defy the spirit of the regulations by hoisting them high in the sky and making them huge in size.

Quasi-monopolies

The ability of business corporations to impose all those costs and other damages to society is facilitated by allowing corporations to grow so large that many are quasi-monopolies. Antitrust principles have been largely diluted or ignored in recent years in the United States and elsewhere. One of the most ominous consolidations is in communications. "With this control," says Bradley Stillman, Consumer Federation of America, "comes the ability to influence political discourse and shape our national culture."

Corporate Excuses

It is not very useful to try to judge how well developed is the value system of most businessmen and how sensitive they are to what is fair and unfair. Many businessmen conceal this especially whey they can justify wrongdoing by truthfully asserting it is legal. Too often they try to justify other wrongdoing by resorting to the stance "nolo contendere" – paying the fine, claiming innocence, and using the excuse they don't want to take the time and money in court to defend their positions. A basic defect is that most corporate decisions are made by unelected persons secretly behind closed doors.

Problem Structural As Well As Ethical

Alongside the illustrative list of corporate wrongdoing could be noted many examples of responsible actions by corporation officers in addition to their conventional practice of producing useful goods and services. However, even if all corporations became fairer in such policies as labor relations, a sustainable environment, and public disclosure, it would not suffice. The whole system needs reorientation. The present world order of globalization, as Tony Clarke points out, "has been designed to protect the rights and freedoms of transnational capital . . . for efficient transnational competition and profitable investment." That must be subordinated, he continues, to the much higher priority of "the basic human and democratic rights of people." This requires major shifts of power as well as structural political, social, and economic change.

COMPLAINTS OF CIVIC LEADERS

It is the above kinds of dissatisfaction, uncorrected by government, that has led so many voters to stay away from the polls. Votes no longer determine how power and money are applied, they say. How near we are to a crisis may be discerned by noting the complaints of many civic leaders crying out their frustrations and then announcing default or humiliating concession. Consider these five recognitions of major political-social barriers:

(1) Fred Wertheimer, president for 14 years of the 250,000-member Common Cause organization which lobbies in the public interest, has long charged bluntly that the system for financing Congressional election campaigns is "corrupt." He spoke to the *Washington Post* in October 1995 of "very deep" cynicism about reform by Congress and the President and announced his plan to resign his position at Common Cause.

(2) Sierra Club executive director Carl Pope, in a full-page newspaper advertisement, said the distance between Capitol Hill and the people is so great that "I often feel as though I live in two countries." He was told by Washington officialdom that the majority of the electorate who want environmental quality are unable to get it because Congress and the President "cannot stand up to money" –

the influential dollars of corporate managers who insist on their right to continue pollution. The result, concluded Pope, is that, "People don't think the federal government represents them and they don't trust it."

(3) Workers are faced with the harsh realities that management controls their jobs, unemployment rates of 6 percent or higher are widely accepted to limit inflation, and union leadership is declining in influence as it rigidly clings to obsolescent concepts of labor-management relationships. According to a sample poll by professors Richard Freeman and Joel Rogers, published by the *Washington Post*, 40 percent of the workers interviewed said they would prefer belonging to a union but were resigned to accepting nonunion labor-management committees. The kind of committee they are being offered provides workers an independent voice and participation in initial decision-making, but concedes to management continued exercise of final control.

(4) Ralph Nader, as head of the Public Citizen organization, declared in February 1992 that a "selfish oligarchy" in the United States has debased politics and caused "the exclusion of citizens from the strengthening of their democracy and political economy. . . . This rule of the self-serving few over the Nation's business and politics has concentrated power, money, greed, and corruption far beyond the control or accountability of citizens." [Under these circumstances,] "poverty, discrimination, joblessness, and the troubled condition of education, environment, street and suite crime, budget deficits, costly and inadequate health care, and energy boondoggles [cannot be] addressed constructively and enduringly." Nader then presented some "Concord Principles" in the conviction that "Our 19th century democratic rights need retooling for the proper exercise of our responsibilities as citizens in the 21st century."

(5) "Political problem solving is today too complex and many-sided a process to be satisfactorily left to political leaders, government or any large system alone," states Harry C. Boyte, senior fellow, Hubert H. Humphrey Institute of Public Affairs. Yet, he adds, Americans have allowed the government-citizen relationship to become largely an expert-client relationship. People are misguided, he believes, by assuming "that the citizens' main role is

to pressure government officials to act, rather than to take action."
The result is "civic crisis," Boyte says, because it does not sufficiently "involve citizens as public problem solvers."

NEED TO AMEND THE CONSTITUTION

The only sure way the people can exercise their sovereignty to supplement representative government with direct democracy, to
terminate buying of Congressional elections by the wealthy, and otherwise effectively to regulate corporations is to amend the
Constitution. The initial amendments proposed here to provide for
referendums and to reform business corporation practices cover the
most basic and urgent changes. Seven provisions seem essential at the
outset for the immediate public good and to redistribute power in
society sufficiently to make other moves toward better government
and economic democracy possible at later times. These needs are:

(1) Initiative and referendum
     To require state governments, whenever petitioned by regis-
     tered voters equal in number to 5 percent of the ballots cast in
     the latest major election, to place national initiatives on the bal-
     lot for a referendum vote, provided the proposition is made
     public for debate five months prior to voting. Any such initia-
     tive, when passed by a majority of voters in two-thirds of the
     states, shall become national law amending any preceding law.

(2) Content of corporation charters
     All business corporation charters shall be recalled without enti-
     tlement to compensation and shall be replaced by new charters
     issued by the national government. The new charters will have
     strict anti-trust provisions, recognize the right of employees to
     organize unions, require that operations abroad conform to the
     same constraints as required by law for domestic operations,
     require that all corporate lobbying of national and state govern-
     ments be performed in public and be a matter of public record,
     and that all contracts have a cooling off period of one week
     during which any party many withdraw without penalty.

(3) Rights of corporations
Any claim or interpretation that a corporation or other organization is a person or has the rights of a person in legal and other matters is invalid.

(4) Size of business corporations
Business corporations shall be divided, within one year of ratification of this amendment, so that no entities have more than 10,000 employees.

(5) Membership of board of directors
The number of directors in all business corporations shall be divisible by three, so that one-third shall be shareholders, one-third employees, and one-third community representatives. Management employees are ineligible for board of director membership. Voting in the boards of all business corporations shall be on the basis of one director/one vote, without regard to the amount of stock held.

(6) Corporation election contributions
All business corporations are prohibited from contributing to the election campaigns of any candidate, party, initiative, or referendum, directly or indirectly.

(7) Organizational gifts to candidates
All business corporations and other organizations are prohibited from presenting gifts (including honoraria for speeches or royalties for writings) to political candidates or officeholders.

The call "to reconfigure corporate governance" has notably been made by Fred Block.

RATIFICATION

In amending the U. S. Constitution – after proposals, drafting, and dialogue have been run their course – the manner of ratification then needs to be arranged. Article V specifies that ratification be "by the legislatures of three-fourths of the several States, or by conventions in three-fourths thereof, as the one or the other mode of ratification may be proposed by the Congress." The last clause of that quotation is curious and insignificant. If Congress or any other organization or person proposes that state legislatures consider ratification and if the proposal is followed and that ratification fails, the people are still free to elect representatives to special constitutional conventions to consider ratification. Furthermore, the conventions are superior to and not bound by the Constitution, may change the conditions (including the number of approving states required) for ratification, and have the function of making law – unrestrained by any government – in the form of constitutions instructing governments.

It is worth repeating that the fact that the original U. S. Constitution was ratified by the states does not mean it was ratified by the state legislatures. It was not. It was ratified, as the members of the Constitutional Convention advised, by special state conventions established for that single purpose. Representatives to those conventions were elected directly by the people. William Peters states that James Madison distrusted the state legislatures for that function and differed strongly with those who favored ratification by legislatures. Madison, Peters says, thought it "indispensable that the new constitution should be ratified in the most unexceptionable form and by the supreme authority of the people themselves."

Recognizing the essentiality of this procedure, Alexander Hamilton in the conclusion of *The Federalist* paper No. 22 spoke of "the necessity of laying the foundations of our national government deeper than in the mere sanction of delegated authority. The fabric of American empire ought to rest on the solid basis of THE CONSENT OF THE PEOPLE. The streams of national power ought to flow immediately from that pure, original fountain of all legitimate authority."

Ratification could be, as an alternative to special convention, by referendum.

6

POWERS REDELEGATED
TO STATES AND COMMUNITIES

The present U. S. Constitution is unsatisfactory primarily because it delegates too many powers to the national government. Many of those powers should be redelegated to local governments or to a new transnational government or retained by the people. Certain powers that should remain at the national government level are in need of redefinition.

FEDERALISM

The overriding principle involved in delegation of power is federalism. The word originally meant merely the joining by treaty of two or more sovereign entities in what is usually now called a league, alliance, or confederation. Later the term federalism referred most often to a political system where various powers were assigned to a variety of specific bodies in a single state. Now the term federalism conventionally refers to the kind of government where the sovereign people, usually by means of a written constitution, specify which powers are delegated to various parts of government – transnational, national, state, and local – and which powers are retained by the people.

The idea of federalism was propounded principally by James Harrington, John Milton, Thomas Paine, James Wilson, and James Madison. The reasons usually given for its development were the deficiencies in confederations, namely, that they are agreements with no means of enforcement except voluntary national action, and are without direct relationships with individual persons. Yet remedies for those deficiencies could be built into confederations as well as federations. A unique feature of a federal government is subsidiarity – delegation of various powers in each case to that part of government which is closest to the sovereign people and able to exercise those powers toward effective and agreeable ends. The term subsidiarity conventionally assigns powers to the "lowest" appropriate "level" of government, but those two terms imply erroneously that a federation is a hierarchy of different levels of government; it is not.

The first government to adopt the federal principle, in its modern sense, was the United States of America. Among the federal governments which followed successively were those of Belgium, Argentina, Canada, Switzerland, Australia, Mexico, Germany, India, Brazil, Russia, and South Africa.

With reference to kinds of government, it is helpful to set definitions of the terms involved. Local government, to be specific even if arbitrary, should not include state or provincial governments but rather be comprised of county and town governments and also community and neighborhood civic associations. Sovereignty, again to sharpen the specificity of the term even if arbitrary, should be restricted to mean ultimate or constituent sovereignty and residing in no government but only in the people as an electorate. Constituent means the authority to legalize constitutions. Responsibilities temporarily assigned by sovereign people through constitutions to various parts of government should be called delegated powers or simply powers. Various governments – local, state, national, and transnational – are more properly termed parts rather than levels of government. They are best conceived of as beside each other rather than in a hierarchical vertical position where one is above another. Although there are relationships between various parts of government, one part of government in a democratic federation does not instruct another part. It is the sovereign people who delegate specific powers to each part of government, side by side, as diagrammed in Figure 1.

To provide a perspective as to the size of various parts of government in the United States, the Census Bureau reports these figures on employment and expenditures:

Parts of government	Number of public employees in 1992	Expenditures in FY 1992
Local government	11 million	$ 648 billion
State government	5	$ 499
National government	3	$1,341
Total	19	$2,488

American citizens surprisingly have never established any formal way for determining what share of taxes shall be charged by each part of their governments or what share of expenditures shall be made by each part. The procedure and results are rather ad hoc. A major adjustment occurs when the national government transfers funds to state governments in block grants, ostensibly so the national government can attach conditions promoting fair use of the money. Of total U. S. public expenditures in FY 1992, about 26 percent was by local governments, 20 percent by state governments, and 54 percent by the national government (figures based largely on U. S. Bureau of the Census data). With regard to costs of one U. S. health program, Medicaid, state governments in a recent year paid 43 percent and the national government 57 percent.

DECENTRALIZATION

It stands to reason that many government activities could best be planned and managed in or near the localities where they operate. Knowledge about the activities is apt to be greatest there, and – even more important – the effects of those activities on people, either benefits or harm, are most apparent there. Yet national governments in every country have overcentralized their control of public affairs and erased much of the essential touch between the governed and the governors. It is time drastically to decentralize.

A proposed constitutional amendment (here numbered 8 following the seven proposed in Chapter 5) follows:

(8) Distribution of powers between nation and localities
The principal government responsibility in health, education,

social services, public safety, housing, and public works is to reside in state and local governments. The proper role of national government in those sectors is confined to setting standards, equalizing opportunities, and evaluating performance. Governments should keep police departments, prisons, and parks under public management and prohibit privatization of them.

Proposed returns to "state's rights," however, bring forth reasonable objections or, at least, apprehensions. "The phrase was a frightening symbol of injustice" during 1935-65, states journalist Carl T. Rowan. Continuing, he says, "It symbolized the right of Tennessee to segregate me in an inferior public school, to deny me the right to read a book in my town's only public library, to declare me unfit to get a drink of water in a 'white' drugstore, or to sit in the city park or to enter the town's hotels except as a bellhop."

Little is more important than to be reminded thus of the failure of many states and towns to protect civil liberties in the not so distant past. Now we must judge how much progress has been made since then. It is commonly held that the advance of justice has been great, but Rowan believes some states "will not only cut unfavored people off life-and-death programs but will divert federal funds to their cronies and self-enriching projects." So both the past and even part of the present are unacceptable as regards racial equality. However if citizens do become determined to put in place a fairer society, they may have more access and greater chances of effectiveness in most of their own communities rather than in faraway national offices. Federal standards, evaluation, and court proceedings, however, must be preserved.

Decentralization is commendably a major policy objective of most of the Republicans who won the majority in Congress in 1994. Two of their analytical spokesmen, William Eggers and John O'Leary of the Reason Foundation in Los Angeles, are confident the decentralization movement, which they call a "devolution revolution," is well on its way. They state it "is not a partisan issue." Eggers and O'Leary are at their best in diagnosing some of the faults of the status quo and looking to civil society (their "third pillar") for much of the remedy. They largely ignore, however, what to do about the great problems of disadvantaged human beings likely to be bypassed by decentralization and how to handle irresponsible business corporate power. Their constructive analysis is marred by inclusion of reactionary recommendations to give Western residents the Western land and other resources belonging to all Americans and to compel taxpayers to reward land owners for any inconvenience (which they label "takings") resulting from their duty to obey environmental, health, and safety laws.

STATE GOVERNMENTS

Sixty-four percent of 1,003 respondents in a 1995 poll on government responsibility favored a shift of power from national to state authorities. The poll was conducted by Peter Hart and Robert Teeter for the Council for Excellence in Government, as reported by Guy Gugliotta. In similar vein, Republican governors meeting at Williamsburg, Va. in November 1994 stated they were seeking "a significant shift in power and responsibility from Washington to the states," reported Dan Balz.

In recent decades, states in the United States appreciably lengthened legislature sessions, increased the size and professional qualifications of their agency and legislative staffs, and elected better-educated governors to longer terms. As a result, according to former federal budget director Alice M. Rivlin, the states have proven they are far more efficient at raising revenue and holding down expenses than Washington.

"States are in strong financial shape and probably will not feel the effects of [cuts in] proposed federal spending for several years. . . . [but] the budget good times are not expected to last," concluded the National Governors' Association and the National Association of State Budget Officers in a 1995 report analyzed by the Associated Press. That recognizes the likelihood that states will be receiving less federal funds while their responsibilities are increasing. Part of the matter was addressed on March 22, 1995, when a Congressional bill was signed mandating federal funds to accompany new federal requirements on states in many instances. The law exempts, however, application in anti-discrimination matters, the most common kind of mandate in recent years, according to Ann Devroy and Helen Dewar.

A complicated related question is what proportion of state/local expenditure should be covered by state/local revenues and what by federal revenues. Some block grants from the national government to states may be appropriate to give it leverage to carry out its function of equalizing opportunities throughout the country. However, the block-grant procedure is usually faulty in being laden with bureaucratic burdens on the recipient state to file and receive approval of program plans and implementation procedures. In view of the facts that states have unequal resources and consequent taxabilities, Rivlin proposes "common shared taxes." That procedure would involve identical taxes in each state and division of the revenues on a per-capita basis. In Germany, uniform income taxes are levied on all citizens and corporations and the proceeds shared by the federal, provincial (Lander), and local parts of government.

CITIES

Discussion of decentralization of some national government management to the city level is being heard especially from businessmen. Demands for greater autonomy for cities, reports William Drozdiak, are coming especially from European ones which feel they have more in common with foreign cities than with their own capital cities and national governments. Entrepreneurs are realizing that combining research, financial facilities, and markets makes networks of cities the center of job creation and prosperity. Faster rail connections and the need to coordinate environmental policies accentuate the trend. It has brought Lyon, Geneva, and Turin – across three national borders – into an Alpine Diamond alliance. Lyon, Stuttgart, Barcelona, and Milan, known as the Four Motors, Drozdiak continues, "have started bypassing their national governments and meeting on their own to explore new avenues of cooperation."

COMMUNITIES

For many public activities, including social services, education, and public safety, even state government is too centralized. The principal aspects of those activities warrant the attention of county and town governments. "'Power to the Governors' or 'Power to the Mayors' is not exactly the same thing as 'Power to the People,'" says journalist E. J. Dionne Jr. So there is also an important role for non-government community organizations, neighborhood meetings, and individual citizens.

"The price to be paid for eliminating intrusive, top-heavy government in Washington is increased responsibility at the community level. And that in turn demands a more engaged citizenry," comments David S. Broder. Similarly, Wendell Berry, as reported by Scott M. Morris, says "A commitment to a locality is a commitment to being rooted, which in turn demands responsibility. It is in fulfilling such obligations that our humanity flowers."

Significant activity in civil society, between government and market on the one hand and individualism on the other, does operate at the community level. Amitai Etzioni, professor at George Washington University, is the leader of a so-called communitarian movement to invigorate this activity. He believes the family, school, and community should be the prime transmitters of moral values. He calls for town meetings and social bonds leading to family support, community service, and the social obligations we have to each other.

Among the organizations composing the movement of communitarians and other local-action-oriented people in the United States are four cited by David S. Broder: Alliance for National Renewal / National Civic League, collaborating with John Gardner; the New Citizenship Project, funded by the Bradley Foundation of Milwaukee; the American Civic Forum, led by Professor Harry C. Boyte of the University of Minnesota and William Galston, an aide of President Clinton; and the Center for Civic Education, directed by Charles N. Quigley. As organizations such as these become more influential, special interests (well defined by Paul Jensen and Peter Henle as anyone's interests but yours) may find it more realistic to plead their causes in town meetings rather than before government representatives and officials. Open dialogue among citizens could become more influential on future legislation than private conversations between individuals

and representatives, especially after fundgiving and other induce-
ments of lobbyists are largely outlawed.

Probably the most effective organization lobbying in the public
interest on a wide variety of issues is 20/20 Vision. The target of its
lobbying is principally the Congress and occasionally the President,
a cabinet officer, or agency director. However, 20/20 Vision has
strong grass-roots characteristics in that the lobbying is done mainly by citizens organized in Congressional districts throughout the
country. Furthermore, sometimes the lobbying is directed toward
state governments or local newspaper readers. 20/20 Vision operates typically by asking citizen subscribers to pay $20 a year to
receive monthly a timely issues postcard providing information
helpful in spending 20 minutes to write a letter of opinion to a representative about some pending legislative bill. The cards are
written and mailed by core groups in each district. The expert
information and opinions about issues and legislative timetables are
obtained by a proficient backstopping office in Washington, DC.,
directed by Robin Caiola and Naila Bolus.

Some community action focuses on a single sector, such as public
safety. Although there has been an explosion of get-tough laws and
official policies, John Anner describes "community groups that
want to find more humane and just solutions to community public
safety problems." Two distinct kinds of such activism are
Neighborhood Watch and anti-crime councils collaborating with
local police on the one hand, and groups like the Greensboro
Justice Fund (in North Carolina and nationwide), Justice Denied
(in Maryland), and Justice for Jarrold Hall (in California) protesting
improper police and court action on the other hand.

Created to integrate both of the above approaches is the
Campaign for Community Safety and Police Accountability
(CCSPA). It is led by the 15-year-old Center for Third World
Organizing, Oakland, Cal., which operates strategy and research
centers. Its four basic principles, Anner continues, are "crime prevention through reallocation of resources to social needs and
conflict resolution; promoting community justice and alternatives
to incarceration; fostering public participation; and police accountability to the community." He quotes CCSPA member Robbie

Smith stating that, "Prevention is the key. We have got to find things for kids to do before they get in trouble." A potential source of funds for prevention programs is the assets seized in drug raids, estimated at $7 billion in 1984-95. Usual practice is for police departments to allocate most of the money. However, the CCSPA is working in many places to try to get much of it allotted to crime prevention. As a modest help, U. S. Department of Justice regulations now allow 15 percent of asset forfeiture proceeds to be used for that purpose.

Another single sector appropriate for community-action attention is social welfare. Opinions differ, of course, as to the relative roles of government and community. "States have been in something of a race to lower welfare benefits for fear that high benefits could attract poor people to the state – thus raising social spending and perhaps triggering an exodus of taxpayers," said Harvard Professor Paul E. Peterson as quoted by Judith Havemann. The latter mentioned two additional scholars questioning the moving of welfare problems to states to solve, but their objections largely focused on using the not necessary procedure of block grants.

As regards welfare, William Raspberry reports the views of Robert L. Woodson, Sr., president, National Center for Neighborhood Enterprise and head of a task force created in 1995 by House Speaker Newt Gingrich. Woodson believes, "The primary providers of services ought to be the peers of those receiving the services, living in the same zip code." He acknowledges "the difficulty of freeing the uncredentialed local geniuses to do their wonderful work without opening the door for unconscionable frauds to do theirs." Wary of most government regulation but not against standards, Woodson seeks a middle ground. He calls it "real devolution – moving the certification, the oversight and the funding authority as close as possible to the community being served."

The greatest single-sector political activity at the local level is concern about various aspects of the environment. The Sierra Club, the Greens, and the National Audubon Society have active chapters throughout the country promoting conservation. Business corporations opposing environmental regulations also have set up numerous organizations – usually with titles deceptively implying conservational or grass-roots citizen orientation – including the Abundant Wildlife Society, Alliance for Environment and Resources, Citizens for the Environment, Environmental Conservaton Organization, Fairness to Land Owners Committee, and the Wilderness Impact Research Foundation. Some of these business-oriented groups claim the right to use their land in any way they see fit with little or no responsibility to society. They call themselves a "wise use" movement. The most extremist of these business and individual people, living mainly in Western United States, claim such rights on public lands actually belonging to all citizens. They have organized such groups as People for the West, Sagebrush Rebellion, and the County Supremacy Movement. Even though the public lands in the West have at no time belonged to Western states, more than 70 rural Western counties have passed or proposed laws to "take back" the public lands, according to Christopher A. Wood. Ugly events related to this movement in 1994-95 were three bombings of federal Land Management and National Forest buildings in Nevada and death threats against federal wildlife employees in New Mexico and Oregon, as reported by Susan Schmidt.

Sometimes an unlikely coalition advances conservation. The "Green Scissors" project, advanced by Friends of the Earth and the National Taxpayers Union Foundation in 1995, detailed $33 billion in federal spending it found "environmentally and fiscally wasteful," according to Tom Kenworthy. Among eliminations the project called for were subsidies to mining companies on public lands, construction of roads in national forests for use by lumber companies, and proposed building of an Animas-LaPlata dam in Colorado.

"Although enthusiasm for environmental protection is waning in Washington, local environmental activists report that it is rising in other parts of the country," says Gary Lee. He emphasized the point by quoting Mary Alice Brooks, head of the Lee Seville Miles Citizen Council in Cleveland, Ohio, who said in 1995, "Local residents are working for the environment on many fronts. . . . But the gap between local activism and environmental politics in Washington is glaring. . . . The grass-roots sector is the only one fighting these issues." At the same time, the National Academy of

Public Administration, in a report sponsored by Congress, recommended that more authority to fight pollution should be given to states, localities, and some private enterprises.

A grass-roots activity that is strengthening some communities is local-currency exchange. It is a barter system which creates a paying demand for unused skills, services, and land. It expands the buying capabilities of participants in the system beyond the dollars available to them. Payment is in local currency which can be spent only within the community and thus helps prevent jobs being exported. A notable such exchange called LETS was created by Michael Linton in Comox Valley, British Columbia in 1983 and grew to 500 members. Its unit of currency is called the green dollar, and amounts owed to or by each participant exist as records kept on paper or in a computer database. There are nearly 200 local exchanges like LETS in Britain and 21 in the United States, says Susan Meeker-Lowry. She gives examples of services offered through directories to anyone willing to pay in local currency: In Britain, "bicycle and car maintenance, music and language lessons, gardening, child-care, food and food processing, craftwork, manual labor, message, and many other resources." In Ithaca, NY, "rent, plumbing, carpentry, car repair, chiropractic, food (two large locally-owned grocery stores as well as farmer's market vendors accept them), firewood, childcare . . . some movie theaters . . . bowling alleys and the local Ben & Jerry's" ice cream shop. The Ithaca local currency unit is called the HOUR, reflecting the interesting practice of participants in the system valuing each other's work at the same currency rate per hour.

Management of community nonprofit organizations are sometimes improved by retired business executives. Frank Pace, former secretary of the Army, founded the Executive Service Corps for that purpose in 1977. It now has 10,000 volunteers who for small fees provide management expertise to community organizations concerned with employment, homeless, hospice, AIDS, student, and other programs, according to Randy Giancaterino. He mentions that one of the groups helped was the 200-year-old Friends Association For Care and Protection of Children in West Chester, Pa., with a staff of 20 people. It began to falter with underfunding, insufficient community awareness and support, and low staff morale. Things turned around to the better when Dale Stone, retired executive from Sun Oil Co., provided recommendations on improved management strategy and procedures.

Citizens, town planners, and architects could make a great contribution to community cohesion if they more often included, near housing developments, some space where residents could walk to and engage in casual conversation. It could be a public square, coffee shop, corner shop, community center, tea garden, tavern, or dance hall, suggests sociologist Ray Oldenburg.

DIVERSITY

An important reason for decentralization is to recognize and support diversity. Every cultural group deserves to have its customs, music, literature, etc. accepted and respected. Where there are major differences in language, religion, education, etc., adjustments become necessary. Yet it is well to avoid the two extreme solutions. Assimilation or homogenization of different groups in a melting pot, on the one hand, is apt to mean repression and disappearance of cultures. Segregation or isolation of groups into a mosaic or patchwork, on the other hand, is usually unwieldy and unfriendly. The commendable attitude is for each group asking and deserving respect for its culture to accord equal respect for other groups, the nation, and humanity as a whole. Federalism facilitates this by the possibility of arranging, for a province such as Quebec, to diminish the unwanted influences of nearby provinces while retaining (or acquiring) linkages on limited matters such as security and trade in a geographically wider union.

Acceptance of diversity is even more significant than a civilized personal attitude. It is also a lubricant of civil society, allowing different viewpoints and procedures to operate simultaneously with a minimum of friction. A profound benefit of this is appreciable lowering of the need for coercion (government or otherwise) to maintain order. Such reasoning leads Inis Claude in social development to seek citizenship even before brotherhood, manageable pluralism before community, and tolerable diversity before unity.

7

POWERS REDELEGATED
TO TRANSNATIONAL GOVERNMENT

Despite the wisdom and benefits of maximizing the decentralization
of government and economies, there are some problems clearly
beyond the capabilities of state or national governments to handle.
This circumstance prevails regardless of the degree of intelligence,
political philosophy, or disposition of the government officeholders.
The principal problems outside of national jurisdictions are war,
international trade, monetary foreign exchange, and global pollution. With the principle of subsidiarity in mind (as discussed in
chapter 6), the only kind of government which could manage those
problems effectively is one which does not now exist – namely, a
law-making government at the transnational level. Therefore it
behooves the people – the only valid sovereigns – to write a constitution either for the world or at least for their respective region
(such as a subcontinent or continent) with limited powers in
defense, trade, currency, and pollution. At the same time, for con-
sistency, the people of each nation would have to amend their
national constitutions to withdraw the limited powers redelegated
to the new regional government. Two of the best books on the pros
and cons of world or regional government are *World Federation?* by
Ronald J. Glossop and *One World or None* by Errol E. Harris.

Not Hierarchical World Government

It is important to note that this is not a proposal for world government in the usual sense of the word which visualizes another layer
of authority on top of national governments. An undesirable
authority of that type would be erected by national governments,
would be hierarchical in nature and ever more indirect and distant
from the people, and would be uncontrolled by a constitution and

oversight by the people. On the contrary, the transnational government proposed here would have no sovereignty whatever, would not be shaped or affected by national governments, and would make laws and operate only under a limited constitution legalized directly by the people and only under oversight directly by the people in special conventions or by referendum. Furthermore, the size of total government would be less, as national governments would be greatly reduced, and the composite services and agencies of the transnational government could avoid countless duplications characteristic of separate nations.

In his search for a public philosophy, Sandel also rejects the usual conception of world government. The most promising alternative to independent nationalism, he says, "is not a one-world community based on the solidarity of humankind, but a multiplicity of communities and political bodies – some more, some less extensive than nations – among which sovereignty is diffused."

NEED FOR TRANSNATIONAL DECISION-MAKING

During the present century 110 million people have died in 250 wars, reports Ruth Leger Sivard. There is no way war and many other world problems can be solved without some form of transnational decision-making. In facing the very real global dangers of nuclear proliferation, advances in biological and chemical warfare, and the sophistication and extent of terrorism, human beings surely will be able to conduct more effective preventive surveillance in transnational unions than in many scattered separate nations. It may require transnational governments to be strong enough to deal effectively with transnational corporations, to arrange economic trade-offs, and to guide global development so as to preserve a self-sustaining environment. When dangerous disputes arise between the leaders of different countries, it has often led to war and can do so again. However, if the countries are linked in a democratic transnational federation, the federal authorities can apprehend individual offenders, and the involved localities are less apt to reach a boiling point or have an effective capability to battle.

North Atlantic Union

The region most nearly ready to consider establishing a transnational government is parts of two subcontinents – Western Europe and northern North America. It is the so-called North Atlantic or Northwestern region. Clarence K. Streit, New York Times correspondent in Geneva, presented in 1939 detailed proposals for a union of peoples experienced in democracy. He recommended that some 300 million United States citizens, British, French, Canadians, Dutch, Belgians, Swedish, Swiss, Danes, Finns, Irish, and Norwegians found a transnational "federal union" government. He also suggested including distant Australians, South Africans, and New Zealanders initially and other peoples worldwide as they became democratic. He excluded, for the time being, Germans and Italians then under the yoke of fascism. The proposal was widely discussed, usually favorably. In 1962 delegates selected by Western European and northern American national legislatures met at Paris as the Atlantic Convention of NATO Nations to explore greater cooperation. Some hoped that the recommendations for a Euro-American transnational government would result, but it was not seriously discussed. In the decades that followed, greater collaboration consisted only of treaties carefully guarding the rights of each nation to continue with full independence to pursue its own "national interest" according to its unilateral determination.

The organization founded by Streit, first called Federal Union and later the Association to Unite the Democracies, Washington, DC, published in 1990 an illustrative constitution tailored to a union of those democracies belonging to one or more existing treaty organizations. Its International Drafting Committee was chaired by Dr. Jane Elligett Leitner. The constitution draft has many characteristics of one which might be fashioned by the people as an electorate, but it ambiguously refers in some places to "member nations" and "member states." A union composed of national governments can be disregarded at any time by a national government member, whereas a union established under a constitution legalized by the people as an electorate is outside the jurisdiction of national governments. The illustrative Leitner document presents a variety of possible memberships, all those of treaty organizations, viz., the North Atlantic Treaty Organization (NATO), European Union (EU), the Organization for Economic Cooperation and Development (OECD), and the Organization for Security and Cooperation in Europe (OSCE). The NATO members correspond closely to the Streit proposal but add Germany, Italy, Turkey, Greece, and Iceland and omit Australia, South Africa, and New Zealand. OECD membership is the same as NATO plus Japan, Mexico, Spain, Australia, Portugal, Austria, New Zealand, and Luxembourg. OSCE is essentially OECD plus Russia, Eastern Europe, and Central Europe. Notably absent in all four groupings are the three-fourths of the world's people who live in the global South – Asia (excluding Japan), Africa, and Latin America. The few exceptions are South Africa in the Streit proposal, Turkey in NATO, Mexico recently added to OECD, and various Asian nations formerly part of the USSR and presumably members of OSCE.

The region most ready to form a union democratic government, as previously noted, is the North Atlantic or Northwestern. It consisted in mid-1995 of 740 million persons. (Population data from U. S. Bureau of the Census, as reported in The World Almanac.) It would be 761 million if Australians and New Zealanders joined, 890 million if Central Europeans joined, and 1016 million if Japanese joined. Possible alternatives are that some Central Europeans might prefer to form a transnational union of their own or join Eastern Europeans, and Japanese might rather unite with other East Asians.

It is fair to acknowledge that the rest of the world well may shudder when North Atlantic peoples integrate politically, for unification would further advantage those already the strongest and richest. However, they also are the most experienced in democracy – a potential influence toward restraint, responsibility, and justice. Nevertheless the "national interest" and economic competitiveness of a North Atlantic union will be something to behold, unless its military and trade policies are consistently enlightened without the slippages too characteristic of present-day national powers.

At Independence Square in Philadelphia on the Fourth of July 1962, President John F. Kennedy declared, "I will say here and now, on this day of Independence, that the United States will be prepared to discuss with a united Europe the ways and means of forming a concrete Atlantic partnership, a mutually beneficial partnership between the new union now emerging in Europe and the old American Union founded here 175 years ago." The president added, the following day at a news conference reported by the New York Times, "We do not want this to be a rich man's club while the rest of the world gets poorer. We want the benefits of this kind of union to be shared." Several decades later former prime minister Margaret Thatcher at Fulton, Missouri on March 9, 1996 called for nurturing an "Atlantic political relationship" between the United States and Western Europe.

AMENDING NATIONAL CONSTITUTIONS

Great regional republics would be more competent and just as free as today's familiar governments. The latter would continue, with a smaller role. A new and wider constitution, parliament, executive, and court would call for the people to innovate and participate in a stronger, fairer, and more prosperous democracy. If or when the people do delegate such regional powers, they would of course simultaneously have to withdraw corresponding powers from their present national governments. A recommended amendment to the U.S. Constitution to accomplish that, numbered 9 here to follow the eight previously proposed - seven in Chapter 5 and one in Chapter 6 - is as follows:

(9) *Distribution of powers nationally and transnationally*
   If or when the people of the United States, Western Europe, and Canada come to believe that providing for their common defense, regulating trade and environmental quality, and issuing a common currency is a sufficiently compelling interest to cause them to write a North Atlantic constitution establishing a transnational North Atlantic government, they will simultaneously repeal the corresponding provisions of their separate national constitutions.

EUROPEAN UNION

The relation of European Union to an Atlantic Union calls for special coordination. Europeans and Northern Americans could form Atlantic Union without any part of federal government between national governments and the new North Atlantic government. On the other hand, if Europeans still want a union with certain powers reflecting their special culture and interests, they could prepare a constitution defining those powers in such a way as to be compatible with a North Atlantic constitution and their respective amended national constitutions. In that case, the part of Europe belonging to European Union would be a new nation within the North Atlantic Union.

Most Europeans realize that their nations cannot do well going it alone and that there is need for new institutions for common action in the European region. As a result, they are building a European Community or Union. But they have not yet decided which of two very different kinds of union they want. One would be limited to being a union of nations, a treaty organization, a confederation, created by bureau officials and diplomats, approved by national governments, and issuing regulations enforceable only by member national governments. The other kind of union would be a union of peoples, a federation, a transnational government, created by representatives elected directly by the people, authorized to make and enforce laws according to a written constitution drafted and ratified by the people. In view of the uncertainty as to which kind of union was wanted, early leaders of the European movement promoted a gradualist functional approach toward the possibility of federation.

The process of creating new European organizations began by integrating coal and steel industries, atomic energy, and trade. The lead-off functional or sectorial organization, the European Coal and Steel Community, was semi-autonomous from the start and advanced competition by introducing price transparency and anti-trust regulations. It also had certain pre-federal characteristics, according to John Pinder, including a High Authority which made policy decisions independent of national governments, an Assembly to which the High Authority was responsible, and recourse to the

European Court of Justice. The new European institutions became progressively more democratic, notably when the Parliament became elected directly by the people, the parliamentarians agreed to represent Europe rather than just their homeland, and the Council changed from consensus decision-making to majority voting on many issues (excluding taxes). The functional and other moves toward integration were strengthened, Pinder points out, by those with special interests in them, such as French and German interests in coal and steel, French and Dutch interests in a common agricultural policy, business interests in a customs union, and British and Dutch interests in budget controls.

The Europeans who wanted to confine integration to treaty organizations completely controlled by national government office-holders were particularly the followers of Charles de Gaulle in France and of Margaret Thatcher in Britain. Their posture is sometimes described as defender of national sovereignty. But it can be only one of pure nationalism to those who see national governments as possessing delegated powers but no sovereignty. The people who are sovereign are free to opt for either unions of nations or unions of peoples, but the latter is obviously more directly democratic.

European federalist leaders during the past half century who favored a union of peoples, although accepting the gradualist functionalist path to it, included Jean Monnet, Robert Schuman, Valery Giscard d'Estaing, Jacques Delors, Francois Mitterrand, Paul-Henri Spaak, Edward Heath, Roy Jenkins, Willy Brandt, Helmut Schmidt, and Helmut Kohl. The federation movement in the European Parliament was pioneered by Altiero Spinelli. He inspired the Parliament to approve in 1984 the Draft Treaty for a European Union. It called for co-decision between the Parliament and Council and decisions by majority vote on legislation, the budget, and appointment of the Commission. It also stipulated that ratification would occur when approved by a majority of member nations containing two-thirds of the population of the Community. The nation states rejected the Draft Treaty and substituted in 1985 the more moderate Single European Act. Spinelli expressed disappointment in the SEA and said it contained nothing new organizationally. He proposed, in the last parliamentary speech before his death in 1986, to discontinue the treaty process and to hold consultative referendums in each Community nation for the European Parliament to draft a European constitution. In contrast to the European treaties adopted so far, a constitution conceivably could provide European institutions with three major shifts in powers – full legislative powers in the Parliament, an independent executive (possibly an outgrowth of the present European Commission) with powers to conduct foreign affairs and military matters for the European Community, and Council (upper house) proceedings held in public.

CHARACTERISTICS OF TRANSNATIONAL GOVERNMENTS

The relationship between size of population and success of a democracy has long been a question. Plato and Aristotle preferred a small state. Machiavelli believed smallness benefitted Sparta and Venice and that largeness was Rome's undoing as a republic. Montesquieu worried that the larger the country the greater diversity of views, aggregates of economic and political power, and consequent disorder. Convinced to the contrary partly by Hume, Madison took the position that larger populations reflecting a variety of interests would be more apt to promote policies based on universal principles and resultant stability.

The advent of transnational governments may be welcomed by certain provinces, ethnic minorities, and other cultural groups which would like to become largely independent from their present nation. Such groups could secede but at the same time utilize membership in a new common transnational government to maintain linkages they would like to keep – such as defense and trade – with the nation of which they were formerly a part. That is, the separating group and the nation from which it detaches would both become provinces of the transnational nation. Each, furthermore, would be free to make inter-provincial (inter-state) compacts with each other on such matters as common waterways, environmental factors crossing borders, and policing.

Among groups wanting more control of their own affairs and

having disagreements with other parts of their nation are: Quebecois, British Columbians, Navajos, and Hawaiians in North America. Scottish, Welsh, and Northern Irish in the United Kingdom. Serbs and other groups in former Yugoslavia. A proposed republic of Padania in northern Italy. Basques and Catalonians in Spain. Corsicans in France. Kurds, Palestinians, Kashmiris, Tibetans, Tamils, and East Timorese in Asia. Biafrans, Southern Sudanese, and Western Saharans in Africa. Some Central and Eastern Europeans who are not yet welcome or do not wish to federate either with European Union or Russia might be more comfortable staying partly separate from those groups but having horizontal links with them by becoming a member of a transnational Northwestern, Central European, or Eastern European/Russian federal union.

The policies over which these separatist groups want greater control (than they have as a minority in a nation) are principally language, religion, education, migration, health care, social services, and celebrations of their particular culture.

TRANSNATIONAL CIVIL SOCIETY

Even though the people have the crucial responsibility of being the sole seat of sovereignty, no single worldwide organization of them – other than the common bond of humanity, acknowledged now and then – is in existence. The United Nations, as we shall discuss later, is a treaty between nations rather than a union of sovereign peoples. The principal non-government and non-business organization that individuals have joined, other than religion, is the political party. They have ordinarily started within a nation, but some have transnational linkages, described by Ralph Goldman. Four transnational parties – Christian Democratic (European People's Party), Socialist, Liberal, and Communist – did major campaigning in the first direct popular election of representatives to the European Parliament in 1979.

A wide variety of private voluntary organizations (PVOs), also less precisely called non-government organizations (NGOs), have been formed in civil society to work in international activities. Like their counterparts mentioned previously in the national context, they include various women's movements, Amnesty International, the Permanent Peoples Tribunal, indigenous peoples' groups, Witness for Peace, the Greens, groups for common heritage of the seas, Antarctica, and space, the World Federalist Movement, and many other organizations – local, national, and transnational in origin.

TRANSNATIONAL MOVEMENTS

The principal organization advocating formation of an Atlantic Union is the Association to Unite the Democracies (AUD), Washington, DC. Founded by Streit, its president is Capt. Tom Hudgens and its manager and editor is Craig Srsen. Present American supporters include former Members of Congress Paul Findley, Eugene McCarthy, and Speaker James Wright; former Tennessee legislator Mary Mize Anderson, former U N deputy-under-secretary-general Robert Muller, Henry Luce III, former National Can Chair Robert Stuart, aeronautics educator Mervin Strickler, college educator James Tipton, and scientist Edward Teller. Americans working toward a federation of democracies are in frequent touch with similar organizations in Canada, Italy, Germany, the United Kingdom, and other European countries.

Another large organization which supports transnational federation in general is the World Federalist Movement, New York city. Some of its members, including Hudgens and Stuart and also Dieter Heinrich, Robert Gaunit, and Menko Rose, are also members of AUD or cooperate with it to advance their shared belief that the best first step toward world federation would be a union of democracies.

Let it be noted, as one ponders the momentous moves to transnational government, that many of the representatives and officeholders in the new institutions will be eminent individuals moving over from existing national and provincial bodies to assume equal or even greater responsibilities.

Different national groups within a continental-size region are more and more frequently asked how they can best relate to each other. This concern increases substantially as transportation and communications become ever faster, as trade gets more involved, and as relations with other continents impact more seriously. Some see this posing the question as to how closely should neighboring nations integrate. Actually there is little choice. Ever-expanding international activities are shoving national groups together. They frequently make momentous decisions about such issues as choice of fighter plane, food policy, exchange rates, and fishery practices. Thus the root question is which is the better of two distinct ways to address political, social, and economic decision-making. We can cling to the present ungainly mix of diplomacy, treaty organizations, and summit meetings. Or the people, more rationally and democratically, can settle international matters through constitutional law enacted by new limited regional governments.

DEEPER LOYALTY TO OUR OWN CULTURES AND ALL HUMANITY

If we do grasp the courage to bring into being a time of political creativity and take such actions as proposed here, we may be inspired by some new loyalties. We can keep – and even deepen - treasured loyalties to our families, our communities, our states or provinces, and our nations. At the same time we could discard the primitive concept of foreigners and learn to welcome as neighbors all others on our continent and even those on other continents. We will not diminish our present loyalties as we develop supplementary ones to our continent and all humanity. When James Wilson was among the disconnected people of the thirteen original American colonies creating a new nation, he is reported by Beer to have observed that, "Citizens take to loving the country which they are building."

Although most civil society activity rightly takes place locally, Richard Falk recognizes its wider role and sees "global civil society as a background against which history unfolds." This springs, he notes, from "feelings of species identity" and "a sense of shared human destiny." These can transcend, Falk continues, the "artificial and constraining boundaries [between] race, class, religion, ideology, gender, language, age, civilization."

8

REFORMING NATIONAL CONSTITUTIONS

The most fundamental need on earth is for all societies to reform their national constitutions or, if they are without one, to write and adopt an adequate written constitution. Civil societies, outside of government, are the appropriate initiators and legalizers of the needed new or revamped constitutions.

Popular movements and town meetings have been effective generators of public influence effecting changes in customs and laws. They have been notably successful in expanding voting rights, civil liberties, and environmental improvement. The participant in mass marches, said Martin Luther King Jr. "was no longer a subject of change; he was the active organ of change." Such was not only a movement for equality, Sandel points out, but also empowerment through voluntary collective action. He adds the commendation that, "The civic virtue distinctive to our own time is the capacity to negotiate our way among the sometimes overlapping, sometimes conflicting obligations that claim us, and to live with the tension to which multiple loyalties give rise."

The private voluntary agencies in global society have their own specialized reasons for being. In addition, they supplement, challenge, and try to change national governments and international government agencies.

The question sometimes arises as to what to do about government actions which some persons and PVOs consider unethical. Henry David Thoreau, in his 1849 essay on Civil Disobedience, pointed out that what is right may be different than what is law. He added that the difference is particularly crucial when a law "requires you to be the agent of injustice to another." Thoreau's essay is reputed to have influenced Gandhi. PVOs which have sometimes encouraged illegal nonviolent resistance include Liberation Theology, Sanctuary for Refugees, English women's occupation of area around Greenham Common cruise missile base, Ground Zero group blockading submarine base at Bangor, Washington, and Greenpeace. Similar illegal actions are the informal enterprises in Peru described by De Soto, the secrecy violations by Ellsberg in releasing official papers about the Viet-Nam War, and treehugging to prevent deforestation.

Political parties, private voluntary organizations, and other groups in civil society seldom give serious consideration to making and amending national constitutions. Yet in their hands is the most appropriate place in which to begin the process. It is the precious responsibility of individuals, who care enough about freedom and justice to join with some grouping of their citizens in civil society, to transmit to our governments the revised instructions for which they stand in such great need.

United States Constitution

The Constitution of the United States is over two hundred years old. Its longevity demonstrates its fundamental worthiness. Yet our nation is hobbled by serious defects in the Constitution, especially many perpetuated deficiencies and failures to progress with the changing times. The founding fathers in a new country of four million people had no inkling of the huge bureaucracies to be built by the national and state governments, of the overriding power – big business – to emerge, of the capabilities of foreign powers to influence our lives, and of the degradation of our environment. Since our founders could not foresee these momentous changes in the world, their Constitution made little provision for addressing them.

As the nineteenth and twentieth centuries unfolded, the emerging challenges were fortunately matched by the increase, education, and civic organization of millions of citizens. They do have the ability and the motivation drastically to improve society by reforming the Constitution. Their readiness to do so is suggested by a report that the portion of Americans who trusted the federal government to do what is right all or most of the time declined from three-fourths in the mid-1960s to only 19 percent in 1994, according to a

Gallup poll. Obviously that government needs new and more comprehensive instructions from the sovereign people.

Between 1789, when the U. S. Constitution went into effect, and now, more than 10,000 proposals for amendment were introduced into Congress, according to Bernstein. Of those, 33 were approved by Congress and 27 were ratified by the states. The six not ratified included most recently equal rights for women and statehood for the District of Columbia. The movement for the former of the two proposals was described by Mary Frances Berry. Of the 27 amendments which have come into effect, 11 embodied the bill of rights (including Amendment XIV prohibiting state infringements of them); 1 outlawed slavery; 5 expanded citizen voting, without regard to race, sex, or tax payment, and extended such voting to Senators and to allow persons aged 18 to 20 to vote; 1 authorized income taxes; 7 were procedural or technical; and 2 enacted and then repealed prohibition against intoxicating liquors.

Adequacy of the Constitution and often-cited problems about its structure and policies are analyzed by James Sundquist of Brookings Institution. His review of possible changes focuses mainly on broad issues such as separation of powers, checks and balances, and relations between Congress and the president. "This book must end," Sundquist concludes, "on a pessimistic note. Nothing is likely to happen short of crisis – which is, of course, the case with all fundamental constitutional reform, in every country of the world and throughout history."

There are a great many highly desirable laws which cannot be enacted in the United States as long as obsolete parts of the Constitution remain unchanged. Those laws would be unconstitutional (either contradicting it or based on rights unspecified in the constitution) or are certain to be blocked by constitutionally-protected expenditures on election campaigns. Removal of those obstacles requires constitutional amendment. Proposals for nine amendments have already been made here – one for referendum (Chapter 5), six for business corporation reform (Chapter 5), one for decentralization (Chapter 6), and one for a North Atlantic Union (Chapter 7). Fifty other amendments are about to be recommended here, beginning with the sequential number 10. They have to do with human rights, employee rights, voting procedure, Congress, the Presidency, national defense, environment and resources, property, business-government collusion, and international relations. Many of these fifty-nine proposals (although drafted independently at an earlier date) parallel the "Principles of Unity" of the Independent Progressive Politics Network, which cooperates with the Green Movement. Many of the proposals also are similar to ones made by Ronnie Dugger, founding editor of *The Texas Observer*, in his landmark article in *The Nation* in 1995. Some of the proposals are among the "Principles" of the New Party and in the alternative political platforms published by *In These Times*.

HUMAN RIGHTS

10. Social Security
A social security annuity system is to be continued by the national government for retired persons, expanded to cover all persons without other means of adequate income. Privatization of that system is prohibited.

11. Discrimination
There shall be no discrimination as to gender, race, ethnic origin, or sexual orientation in employing personnel, setting pay rates, opportunity for advancement, registering in educational institutions, selling housing, assigning child custody, or establishing insurance rates. However, assignment of duties and locations may vary to correspond with different physical characteristics. Affirmative action by employers, educational registrars, contracting administrators, and others should not entail quotas based specifically or directly on sex, race, or ethnic origins. However, no government may consider as reverse discrimination or prohibit qualification ratings, for entry to schools and jobs and eligibility for business contracts, which to an appreciable degree make adjustments for applicant childhoods characterized by limited learning, narrow experience, and unhealthy environments. No government may prohibit any kind of sexual practice in privacy among consenting adults regardless of whether married or not.

12. *Church and State*

The principle of separation of church and state is absolute. Among pertinent prohibitions to Congress and all government officeholders are the authorization, funding, or conducting of organized prayer in public schools, censuses or research on religious practices and church attendance, or debates on the role of religion.

13. *Crimes Abroad*

Any act considered a crime within the United States is also considered a crime when committed by Americans outside the United States.

14. *Executions*

Life after birth is an inalienable right. Killing any person by a person, organization, or government for a crime or for any other reason other than self-defense against imminent threat is prohibited.

15. *Health Care*

Congress shall establish an adequate health care single-payer system with automatic universal coverage, financed from taxes and regulated by elected local boards. Privatization of the system is prohibited.

16. *Education*

Public education at public expense shall be universally available from nursery school through the college level. Government vouchers paying for the sending of students to private schools is prohibited.

17. *Handguns*

The right to personal security has higher standing than a right to have a gun or to any interpretation of Amendment II. Possession of handguns and assault guns are prohibited to all persons except authorized police, national guard, and national and transnational armed forces.

18. *Privacy*

Uninvited telephone or electronic calls to private residences for commercial purposes is prohibited. Government agencies are prohibited from distributing information about individuals without the express consent of each individual involved. Any law preventing, defining, or limiting encryption is prohibited.

19. *Birth and Abortion*

A pregnant woman is responsible, under ordinary circumstances, for nurturing her pregnancy to birth. A pregnant women, for reasons of her own, has the sole right – preferably in consultation with family, religious organization, or other support group – to have an abortion with the timing, place, method, and other conditions decided solely by herself. No government may make any law pertaining to abortion.

20. *Legal Aid*

Any person accused of a crime and who lacks sufficient means of their own is entitled to competent legal defense assistance provided by the government without charge. No law may prohibit the Legal Services Corporation from adequate assistance in class action cases.

21. *Sealed Records*

The judicial practice of sealing court records is prohibited. All records of court trials shall be open to the public after termination of trial, except that privacy of endangered testifiers and of victims of sexual crimes may be preserved.

22. *Electronic Censorship*

Messages transmitted electronically on Internet or otherwise may not be classified as illegal on the basis of such vague and imprecise terms as "indecent," "patently offensive," or of not being suitable for children. Technical devices to control viewing by children may be mandated.

EMPLOYEE RIGHTS

23. *Worker Organizations*

Workers, including farm and civil service workers, have a right to organize unions free of employer intimidation, harassment, or penalty. Employer action against union organization is a crime punishable by law. Permanent replacement of employees as a consequence of striking is prohibited.

24. *Minimum Income*

Congress shall establish a minimum wage of $10 an hour (in 1996 dollars), with that amount indexed annually to reflect changing value of the dollar.

25. *Full Employment*

Congress shall create and fund an agency to offer employment at a living salary to any member of the labor force shut out from other private or public employment and thereby guarantee full employment. Quality child care shall be available at public expense to working parents unless one parent can handle the responsibility without subjecting the family to deprivation. Child care centers shall be regulated by elected local boards.

26. *Work Time*

The standard work week shall be 35 hours. The standard vacation period shall be three weeks plus national holidays, all with full pay.

27. *Workplace Health*

When Congress and state legislatures set standards for health and safety at the workplace, they shall at the same time mandate workplace committees of workers and management to monitor those standards and make reports public. [As proposed by Joel Rogers.]

Voting Procedures

28. Facilitating Voter Registration and Voting

States are required to provide opportunities to persons to register for voting by mail, at libraries, and at government agencies, including simultaneous registration when applying for a driver's license. Days of voting shall be confined to Saturday, Sunday, or a national holiday. No official results of voting may be disclosed until polls have closed in Hawaii.

29. Campaign Contributions

Contributions to political campaigns shall be limited to $100 per person (in 1996 dollars) and to persons whose principal residence is in the area represented by the candidate.

30. Representative Senate

The Senate shall consist of one Senator from each state and one additional Senator for each four million people or fraction thereof beyond the first four million people. During the transition from the present Senate, each Senator is entitled to complete her or his term.

31. Proportional Representation

Vote tallying for transnational, national, and state legislatures shall embody the principles of proportional representation.

32. D. C. and Puerto Rico

Citizens of the District of Columbia and of the territory of Puerto Rico are accorded rights of full and equal representation in the House of Representatives and the Senate.

The Congress

33. Filibusters

Cloture, the limiting of debate and the ordering of a vote, can be invoked in Congress by a simple majority. Congress, as an exception to its privilege of establishing its rules of order, is prohibited from placing any other conditions on invoking cloture.

34. *Ombudsman*

No Member of Congress or of its staff may use official time and funds to help individuals and organizations with problems involving government agencies, legislation, or rulings. Such problems may be addressed by an Ombudsman Commission established by the Congress.

35. *Payments to Members*

Members of Congress while in office, as an exception to their privilege of establishing rules of conduct, are ineligible to receive any payments for speeches, writings, or meeting attendance from private sources while in office. All outside income of Members, except dividends and rents from investments owned prior to government service, shall be limited to 15 percent of their salary.

36. *Subsequent Lobbying*

Members of Congress are prohibited from lobbying Congress during the four years following their departure from office.

THE PRESIDENCY

37. *Electing the President*

The President and Vice-President shall be elected by a majority of the total votes cast nationwide. The provisions for an electoral college and for counting majorities by states are hereby repealed.

38. *Presidential War*

The Congress shall automatically impeach any President who wages war without a formal declaration of war by Congress.

39. *Line-Item Veto*

The President has the authority at his own discretion to veto certain provisions of any Congressional bill he subsequently signs into law.

NATIONAL DEFENSE

40. *Size of Armed Forces*
The United States shall reduce its armed forces by at least one-third below 1996 levels and not exceed the newly specified level unless a substantial threat, beyond any hostilities now existing, presents itself.

41. *Weapons of Mass Destruction and Nuclear Power*
Production of nuclear weapons and construction of nuclear power plants are prohibited, at least until dependably safe long-term solutions have been arranged for all related nuclear waste. Meanwhile,the President of the United States shall adjust the national nuclear weapons stockpile so that the number of warheads is never more than three times the number possessed by the rest of the world. He furthermore shall plan to turn over to North Atlantic armed forces, whenever organized, all United States weapons of mass destruction.

ENVIRONMENT AND RESOURCES.

42. *Pollution*
Persons, corporations, and organizations are prohibited from polluting waterways, land, and atmosphere belonging to others or to the public, except as granted temporarily in a license issued by an appropriate government environmental agency, as paid for by the polluter, and as defined in a pollution abatement program approved by the license-issuing agency.

43. *Resource Conservation*
No national or state government may dispose of any public land, parks, forests, or waterways or allow any private sponsorship thereof. Occasional exceptions to this prohibition are permissible as part of exchanges where the public receives private natural resources whose value is at least equal to the public resources relinquished.

44. Resource Subsidies

No national or state government may permit persons, corporations, or other organizations to obtain water, forest products, minerals, or other commodities from public lands or to graze animals on public pastures except where permission is granted by the appropriate government agency and where payments are made to the government at rates no lower than current market prices of comparable private goods and services.

45. Animals

Animals are an elemental part of a world humans did not create. Wildlife and their habitats have weighty inherent worth separate from, and additional to, economic considerations. Raising animals for food, service, or experimentation and the hunting and killing of wildlife shall be regulated to prohibit cruelty to animals. Animal propagation for those purposes, except where environmentally prudent, shall be discouraged.

PROPERTY

46. Wealth Tax

At least 10 percent of federal tax revenues shall come from a tax on wealth (additional to estate and capital gains taxes). The tax shall be only on net worth above $500,000 (in 1996 dollars), and household effects and moderately-priced automobiles shall be excluded from the calculations. [As proposed by Edward Wolff.]

47. Limit to Takings

The taking of private property for public use, for which Amendment V prescribes compensation, applies only where transfers of title are involved. No property owner required by law to conform to environmental, health, and safety regulations is entitled to any compensation for that responsibility and obligation of citizenship.

48. Tidal Zone

The intertidal zone area between low tide and high tide of the U. S. seacoast in residential, park, and rural areas belongs to the public. Any property owners who believe they own any of the intertidal zone are required to relinquish it within one year and are entitled to compensation only for removal or appropriate modification of pertinent structures.

BUSINESS-GOVERNMENT COLLUSION

49. Subsidies and Exemptions

All government subsidies for the production of sugar, milk, peanuts, tobacco, other crops, minerals, and all other commodities shall be reduced by one-third in each of the next three years so as to reach zero by the end of the third year and to remain at zero. Substantial reductions should also be made in other government subsidies and tax deductions.

50. Finance

Congress shall enact legislation increasing the integrity of financial transactions, reducing non-productive speculation, and moving toward democratization of the economy. Regarding financial transactions, Congress shall provide for greater supervision, fuller disclosure, appreciable taxation on transactions, and major worker share in control of pension funds. Congress shall require the Federal Reserve System to broaden substantially its membership beyond bankers, to report publicly its decision-making more promptly and completely, and to accord employment promotion of greater value than inflation control in policy decisions. Community-controlled banks shall be encouraged.

51. Airwaves

The entire electromagnetic spectrum is proclaimed to be public airwaves, and all licenses to use it are hereby recalled, with no compensation for any expected future benefits. The Congress is authorized to provide for the government to retain ownership of the airwaves and to rent at market rates up to 90 percent of it for periods of time never exceeding five years and providing free electioneering airtime for qualified applicants. At least 10 percent of the airwaves are to be reserved for an audience network, managed by the people for town meetings and other public dialogue.

52. *Patents on Life Forms*

No person, corporation, organization, or government shall be granted a patent on any organs, cells, genes, or proteins, whether naturally occurring, genetically altered, or otherwise modified. Any patents which have been issued on life forms are invalid.

53. *Business Espionage*

No espionage by government agencies shall be made available to persons, corporations, or organizations for commercial advantage.

54. *Maximum Income*

Personal income more than 30 times the minimum wage rate shall be taxed at 90 percent. Total national and state estate taxes for that portion of estates greater in value than $5,000,000 (at 1966 prices) shall be 75 percent.

INTERNATIONAL RELATIONS

55. *International Finance*

The United States government shall withdraw its membership · from the International Monetary Fund and the World Bank and recommend a meeting under United Nations auspices to rewrite the Articles of Agreement of the two agencies. The new articles shall regulate corporations in the public interest, promote both social and economic justice, and broaden executive director membership to include community, labor, educational, and political representation superior in number to financial representatives. Votes by directors shall be one person – one vote rather than by amount of capital stock subscribed.

56. *Taxation*

The Congress is directed to levy taxes on international financial transactions, international air travel, and the use of global commons adequately to cover costs of a fair United States contribution to the operating and capital budgets of the United Nations and its successor organizations.

57. *Intervention*

Unilateral military interventions are prohibited. No citizen, member of the national armed forces, employees of an intelligence agency, or any other person may harm a foreign person or intervene in the internal political, military, or economic affairs of a foreign country, except during a state of war declared by a national or transnational legislature. Congress may support intervention by the U. N. or a continental security force to prevent bloodshed, to ensure delivery of humanitarian aid, and to encourage cease-fire and democratic processes. Concealing of intelligence budget appropriation totals and agency subtotals is prohibited.

58. *Trade Agreements*

The President shall, as soon as possible, withdraw United States membership in the World Trade Organization (formerly the General Agreement on Tariffs and Trade) and the North Atlantic Free Trade Agreement. The President is authorized to negotiate replacement or other trade agreements, provided that all such agreements (a) involve no penalties for preservation and improvement of national and state safety, health, labor, and environmental laws, (b) are managed by boards which negotiate trade disputes in public and which have substantial membership from consumer, environmental, and labor organizations, and (c) allow countries without penalty to prohibit import of goods and services produced under working conditions which do not provide enough pay for basic human needs of worker families, endanger the health and safety of workers, or involve child labor or appreciable environment destruction.

59. Arms Exports

The sale of arms shall be controlled by a code of conduct on arms transfers, which prohibits the transfer of arms to governments that are not democratically accountable to the people, abuse the human rights of their citizens, attack other countries, or undermine international efforts to control the flow of arms.

OTHER PROPOSED AMENDMENTS

One issue discussed in recent years as a potential constitutional amendment was prohibition of Congress to enact mandated requirements on states without appropriating implementation funds. It was taken care of in 1995 by Congressional legislation signed by the President. Other issues considered as possible amendments were term limits, mandatory balanced budgets, keeping illegal aliens out of public schools, requirement of two-thirds vote to raise federal taxes, and prohibition of flag desecration. The present author considers those proposals to lack merit. The proposals demonstrate little faith in voters, raise dubious barriers, presume that aliens are not worthy human beings, and revere the cloth of a flag more than spiritual appreciation of a country's heritage.

It is hoped that most or all of the principles involved in the amendments proposed in this book will be incorporated in transnational constitutions when they are written.

One writer who deplores perpetuating the U. S. constitution as an idol is Daniel Lazare. He, in *The Frozen Republic*, commendably recommends Senate membership based on equality of persons rather than equality of states, prohibition of filibusters, and voting by proportional representation. His principal objection to the Constitution, however, is its checks and balances. This, combined with his evident attraction to the British parliamentary system, leads him to propose depositing almost all powers in a virtually unrestrained House of Representatives. Such a House would be able to amend the Constitution at will (or disregard it), be free from a veto-wielding president, and be unjudged by any supreme court. Lazare wants that kind of House because it would get things done.

Unfortunately, his impatience actually appears to be less with the constitution than with democracy itself.

Economics professor Dennis C. Mueller studied many of the world's constitutions and reported his findings in *Constitutional Democracy*. His recommended improvements include vote counting by proportional representation, confining the activities of national representatives to national issues, prohibition of personal possession of handguns, and periodic constitutional conventions with delegates chosen by lot.

REFORMS ADDITIONAL TO AMENDMENTS

After major reform of the U. S. Constitution, politics will be in a superior framework. That will increase the possibility of looking at other grievances which are not appropriately remedied by constitutional amendment but which, within the new framework, political officeholders are more likely to remedy. Congresses, legislatures, presidents, and governors owe it to the people to make progress in these additional ways:

- Strengthen family farms and farm cooperatives, using acreage limitations and residency requirements, as an alternative to agroindustrial corporations. Original public land and public water objectives for small farms should be honored.

- Rewrite tax laws to make them much more progressive, based on ability to pay, and drastically raising the tax rates on the wealthiest 10 percent of payers.

- Establish a humane law-and-order system based on prevention and rehabilitation rather than on vengeance and prisons.

- End the embargo and other ignoble provisions of the United States feud against Cuban citizens.

- Strengthen the passenger rail system and other forms of public transportation.

• Accord major attention to pollution prevention to supplement and eventually largely replace pollution control.

• Strengthen laws protecting wetlands, endangered species, wilderness, and the global commons including oceans and polar regions.

REAPPORTIONMENT OF U. S. PUBLIC BUDGETS

After decisions are made by the people as to the extent to which national powers will be redelegated down to state and local governments and up to a transnational government, there will need to be a major reapportionment of budgets between the four parts of federal government. In general, of traditional national expenditures, it may be expected that about one-half would be transferred to the transnational government and about one-third to state and local governments, leaving one-sixth at the national level. As regards changes in specific sectors, major expenditures in social welfare, education, job training, housing, highways, and economic and community development now made at the national level ought to be transferred to state and local levels, Rivlin recommends as part of a rationale for "dividing the job." Simultaneously, nearly all so-called national defense expenditures should be by the transnational government responsible for security. See Table 1.

CONSOLIDATION OF CONSTITUTIONS

At some appropriate time in future, it would make sense for Europeans and Northern Americans to consolidate their state, national, and transnational constitutions into a single document.

UNITED KINGDOM CONSTITUTION

Constitutions of nations other than the United States are generally beyond the scope of this book. However, it is considered worthwhile to add a short commentary about the United Kingdom in that respect. "British political thinkers . . . Locke, Hume, Paine,

Table 1
Apportionment of U. S. Public Expenditures
(In percent)*

	Trans-national	National	State	Local	Total
1992 (approximate)					
health and education	–	9	7	16	32
income, welfare, housing	–	16	6	2	24
industry, trans., agric.	–	8	6	9	23
defense	–	13	–	–	13
government, general	–	1	2	5	8
Total	**–**	**47**	**21**	**32**	**100**
Reform (approximate)					
health and education	5	2	8	20	35
income, welfare, housing	–	5	10	10	25
industry, trans., agric.	4	2	5	9	20
defense	10	–	–	–	10
government, general	2	1	2	5	10
Total	**21**	**10**	**25**	**44**	**100**

*Excluding interest on debt.

Source: U. S. Bureau of the Census, Statistical Abstract of the United States 1974, tables 464-466, 509. Amounts for transnational estimated by author of this book.

Godwin, and Mill . . . have done more than those of any other nation to help create the modern idea of democracy," believes the London *Economist* (Oct. 22, 1994). Yet, it continues, the British people have a constitutional monarchy with a contradiction – "that an unelected institution, redolent of authority and selected by accident of birth, depends for its legitimacy on the popular will." It believes that will should be tested by a referendum, but that there is "an even stronger case for reforming other parts of the constitution. . . . Britain's basic constitutional defects arise from the excessive

power of the House of Commons and hence of the cabinet. .
. . [That power] is damaging and inefficient, permitting abuse of
power, excessive centralization and a steady erosion in respect for
government. Yet it derives from the royal prerogatives that
Parliament enjoys; it is reinforced by the weaknesses, since 1911, of
the House of Lords as a scrutineer of legislation; it depends on an
electoral system that allows strong majority governments to be chosen by a minority of votes; it is preserved by the lack of a
constitutional court and bill of rights by which the judiciary could
limit over-mighty government; it is protected by the lack of public
access to information. Government actions, and the actions of
agencies appointed by government, are accountable only to the very
Parliament that the government dominates. . . the House of Lords
should be replaced by an elected second chamber."

There is in Britain a blurring of the boundaries between public
office and private business, according to journalist Fred Barbash.
He reported that nearly one-third of the 651 members of the
House of Commons and many of their staff are also employed by
private lobbying firms. He added that six former cabinet ministers
have joined the boards of companies they dealt with during the
privatization process.

Paddy Ashdown, leader of the Liberal Democrats in Britain, said
in 1991 that the Parliament is not sovereign and that only the people are sovereign.

Part III

THE PEOPLE CALLED FOREIGNERS

9

UNITED PEOPLES AND UNITED NATIONS

The United Nations is the only organization representing all of humanity. It has done reasonably well in reducing disease, extending education, providing technical assistance, helping with peacekeeping, and promoting international commerce in its first fifty years. However, its present capacity to help resolve the basic global problems of war, poverty, and pollution is inadequate. Thus we hear the justified widespread call for reforming it.

The most unsatisfactory characteristic of the U. N. is that, as it title indicates, it is an organization of nations rather than of peoples. There are two undesirable consequences: The delegates to the U. N. are diplomats appointed by national governments, pressured by business corporations, and distant from their sovereigns, the people. The other great weakness is that the U. N. Charter is a treaty among nations – each exercising the right to ignore any agreement whenever it wishes – rather than a constitution authorized by the people to instruct governments in making enforceable law.

If everyone on earth were a free citizen, reforming the U. N. would logically entail all sovereign people electing representatives to conventions to draft a constitution for a limited world government. To emphasize the fact that it would not be a creature of national governments, the organization could aptly be called the United Peoples, and its members would be elected directly by the voters worldwide. Unfortunately, only 20 percent of humanity is free and 40 percent partly free, according to Freedom House, New York. So reforming the U. N. at this time means finding ways to strengthening the governing mechanisms of the 60 percent who are free or partly free and improving their relationships to the 40 percent of humanity still living in nations whose governments do not recognize the people's sovereignty.

Any discussion of freedom worldwide leads to the question of whether democracy is a universal goal consistent with human nature. The fact that free political institutions have developed primarily in the West (Europe and northern America) have led many to believe that democratic practices are largely Western inventions and are not very compatible with Asiatic, African, and Latin American traditions. That viewpoint has a kernel of truth but a greater measure of error. It is based on ethnic conceit, incomplete history, and the fact that much self–government in the global South is at the local level where it has been little noticed and only occasionally studied.

Raul S. Manglapus, former senator and foreign minister of the Philippines, mentions Indian villages characterized by "respect for the dignity of the individual, absence of arbitrariness, and availability of remedies against despotic rule." He says Spaniards invading the Philippines found "barangays" settlements with rulers "who rose to power by consensus of the community." Then, quoting anthropologist Peter J. Wilson, he describes in Madagascar the Tsimihety tribe, providing the nation's president, as "fiercely egalitarian. . . . Every village is a voluntary confederacy of households; each has an equal say in local affairs, exercised through the universal Malagasy institution of the 'fukon'olonga' (village assembly)."

IDENTIFYING NINE REGIONS

Although humanity is not yet ready for intimate global integration, it can make very promising intermediate progress with regional integration. Culturally, geographically, and economically the world can well be thought of as subdivided into nine regions as shown in the accompanying box.

The nine regions are shown graphically in Figure 2.

Millions of Persons			
	Total	Free	Partly Free	Not Free
Africans	682	73	158	451
Central Europeans	129	82	33	14
Chinese	1205	–	–	1205
Eastern Asians	746	50	357	339
Indians (Asiatic)	897	–	897	–
Latin Americans	481	74	396	11
Northwesterners	887	824	63	–
Russians and Eastern Europeans	215	–	215	–
Western Asians	389	5	147	237
World Total	5631	1108	2266	2257

Source: Freedom House and U. S. Bureau of the Census, 1994 data.

These groupings have seemed somewhat natural historically as well as geographically. A principal reason for according them even more emphasis and recognition is that each group is a suitable framework for the human beings in them to develop a sense of community across ethnic and national boundaries. As the degree of community advances, integration economically and then politically becomes more possible. Such integration can then makes security, prosperity, and democracy become realities.

INTEGRATING THE NINE REGIONS

The region most advanced in democracy and integration is the Northwestern, consisting of Western Europe, northern North America, Australia, and New Zealand, as discussed in Chapter 7. Japanese may choose to join Northwesterners, as they do in the Organization for Economic Cooperation and Development, or East Asians.

Figure 2

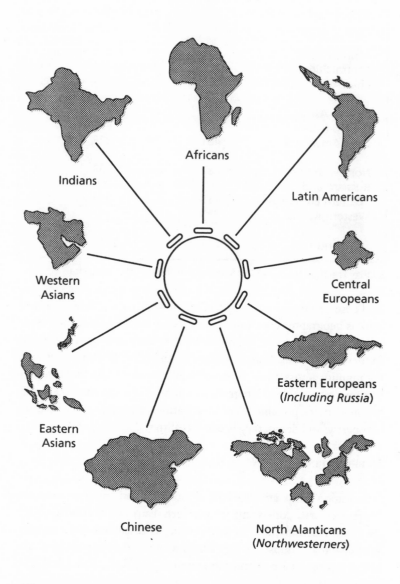

Indians

Africans

Latin Americans

Western
Asians

Central
Europeans

Eastern Europeans
(*Including Russia*)

Eastern
Asians

Chinese

North Alanticans
(*Northwesterners*)

Nine regions proposed for seats on new treaty-making UN Security
and Development Council, replacing present Security Council.

Central Europeans compose the only other of the nine regions which have a majority of fully free peoples. Various groups of them may choose to federate with Northwesterners or Eastern Europeans or organize a separate Central European Union. American nuclear weapons specialist Bruce Blair warns, however, that membership of Central European countries in NATO would likely create anxieties in Russia causing it to deploy from dozens of depots tens of thousands of tactical nuclear weapons along its borders and "represent a serious set-back for operational safety and safeguard against theft." Latin Americans have good prospects for forming a democratic political union. Those of its peoples, recognized by Freedom House as free and thus apt to lead toward integration, are Argentinians, Chileans, Bolivians, and Ecuadorians. The basis for Latin American integration into a political union could be the Organization of American States (presuming the United States gracefully inactivates its participation).

Among Africans, South Africans make up the only large country politically free. Malawians, Malians, Beninians, Sierra Leoneans, Namibians, Botswanians, and Cape Verdeans are also free. They could help the Organization of African Unity integrate into a political community. Russians and Eastern Europeans may federate into a political union, perhaps based on the Commonwealth of Independent States (CIS), founded by Russia, Ukraine, and Belarus in 1991. Moldova and six Asian nations formerly part of the Soviet Union are also members of CIS.

East Asians who are free – South Koreans, Mongolians, and Pacific Islanders – total 50 million persons. Those partly free – Bangladeshi, Philippines, Thais, Taiwanians, Nepalese, Malays, and Sri Lankans – number 357 million persons, according to Freedom House. The two East Asian groups together have 407 million persons who might form a transnational union. Four of those peoples comprising 44 percent of this total are already cooperating in the Association of South East Asian Nations (ASEAN). There is a possibility that the free Japanese, numbering 126 million persons, might initiate or join an East Asian transnational union rather than a union with Northwesterners.

West Asia is not a promising region in which to launch a transnational union at this time, as Freedom House views none of the peoples there as free except Israelis. Those partly free include Pakastanis, Turks, Kirghizs, Jordanians, and Kuwaiti. These six peoples number 215 million persons. They would be reduced to 152 million persons if Turks alternatively chose to unite with Northwesterners as they do in NATO. A dozen West Asian countries sometimes act together in the Arab League, but two–thirds of the people in that organization are North Africans and its capital is in Cairo.

The other two groups of people being discussed here are Indians and Chinese. As they live in two distinct nations – the former partly free and the latter not free – they are already well integrated even though they need to develop more democratically, socially, and economically. Indians should consider relinquishing Kashmiri and the Chinese should allow Tibetans to go their own way. Kashmiri and Tibetans deserve being somewhat autonomous and considered part of the West Asian region.

REFORMED UNITED NATIONS

It would be well if the nine aforementioned world regions formed organizations which became building blocks of a reformed United Nations. The present U N Security Council could be reshaped as a Security and Development Council with nine seats, one for each of the nine regional organizations. If action by the council were limited to proposals approved by consensus, the number of seats would be inconsequential as long as they were fairly representative. Reshaping of the council would involve combining the present British, French, and United States memberships into a single Northwestern seat, broadening the Russian membership to include Eastern Europeans, continuing the Chinese seat, dissolving the ten nonpermanent seats, and adding one seat for each of the other six regional organizations – Central Europeans, Latin Americans, Indians, Africans, East Asians, and West Africans.

It is proposed that the new Security and Development Council sit nearly continuously. Its three principal functions would be to prepare treaties on security, economics, and environmental matters among nations, to determine policy on U N peacekeeping forces, and to determine policy for U N development, trade, and environmental agencies.

Another important U N reform is for the General Assembly to change its voting system to "The Binding Triad" proposed by Richard Hudson of the Center for War/Peace Studies in New York. The new system would count votes three times – the first, one vote per nation (as now); the second, proportional to population; and the third, proportional to contribution to the U N budget (approximately to GNP). Hudson suggests that any bill which passes the General Assembly by a two–thirds majority in the first count and by a simple majority in the second and third counts would become binding world law. He indicates this procedural change could be made by adding one paragraph to Article 13 of the U N Charter.

A U N Parliamentary Assembly and a permanent international Criminal Court which could try individuals charged with crimes against humanity are two important U N reforms recommended by the World Federalist Movement. Advocacy of the United Nations, including timely payment of dues by each country, is promoted by the United Nations Association USA, New York.

Poverty elimination and a sustainable environment could be greatly assisted by global North–South trade–offs arranged by the new Security and Development Council. These are discussed in the following chapter.

GLOBAL CITIZENSHIP

Although intermediate, regional, and partial approaches to world problem–solving always seem more feasible and reasonable than fully global efforts, the vision of a common humanity keeps reappearing. "We shall not love our corner of the planet less for loving the planet, too, and resisting with all our skill and passion the dangers that would reduce it to ashes," said Adlai Stevenson.

One person, Gary Davis of Vermont, founded the International Registry of World Citizens and signed up 750,000 people from 150 countries. He established a World Service Authority in Washington, DC and issued passports, ID cards, and birth certificates to 250,000 people.

In order to stimulate association between industrial democracies and developing–country democracies, Samuel DePalma, David H. Popper, James R. Huntley, Robert Foulon, and other diplomats conducted during 1985–91 an International Committee for a Community of Democracies. They pointed out the relevance of three kinds of connections – a private citizen network, an association of national governments, and an international institute for research on democracy. Some representatives of the global South said such institutions were urgently needed as a way of helping to consolidate their democratic systems. Endorsers of the effort included President Oscar Arias of Costa Rica, former presidents Jimmy Carter and Gerald Ford of the United States, and prime ministers Seaga, Jugnauth, Bhutto, and Soares of Jamaica, Mauritius, Pakistan, and Portugal, respectively.

The principal organization advocating world government is the World Federalist Movement, headquartered in New York with Sir Peter Ustinov as president and William Pace as executive director. Its United States affiliate is the World Federalist Association, Washington, DC; John B. Anderson is president and Tim Barner executive director.

PROPOSED WORLD CONSTITUTION

A few proposed constitutions for full world government have been drafted. Grenville Clark and Louis B. Sohn revised in 1966 their proposed constitution for a world federation.

The organization with the most comprehensive plan for world government and the most cosmopolitan membership is the World Constitution and Parliament Association (WCPA), Lakewood, Colorado, with Philip Isely as its secretary–general. It organized four sessions of a World Constituent Assembly and three sessions of a Provisional World Parliament during 1968–91. At those meetings a Constitution for a Federation of the Earth was adopted, and a campaign is under way to seek its ratification. The constitution provides for democratic government, disarmament of nations, a common currency, and full employment through credit availability to anyone available for useful work.

The WCPA constitution is based to some extent on the U. S. constitution. However, it includes many substantial alternative or additional provisions. They include a third parliamentary house of counsellors, a five–person board as the executive, the right to secede, prohibition of military conscription, free schooling and medical care, freedom of migration and travel, and an ombudsman.

Twenty–eight eminent persons of international standing participated in a Commission on Global Governance, co–chaired by Ingvar Carlsson and Sir Shridath Ramphal, in 1995. Its report, entitled "Our Global Neighborhood," was a perceptive analysis of international problems but its recommendations of what to do about them were only somewhat useful. Commission members did not come to grips with the fundamental problem – the anarchy of nation states. They apparently concluded it was not appropriate to consider government with worldwide jurisdiction at this time because so many people have not yet achieved democracy even within national boundaries and because considerable military power is in the hands of China and a dozen other authoritarian nations which appear opposed to really effective peace and freedom negotiations.

10

FAIRER WORLD

Our founding fathers, along with their remarkable wisdom and virtue, condoned slavery, denial of voting to women and others, massacre of Indians, and stealing Indian land. They viewed with little criticism their European contemporaries plundering Central and South America and other foreign lands. There have, of course, been vast advances in civilization since that time. Usually not noticed, however, is that the well-to-do people in the world have gone little more than halfway in giving up slavery.

It is no exaggeration to say that most international trade between the Northern and Southern continents is based on semi-slavery. More than one billion persons exist in poverty in Asia, Africa, and Latin America – the global South. Almost every one of them is hungry, ill, and little schooled. Part of the cause of such penury is limited access to natural resources – fertile soil, fresh water, forests, minerals, and fisheries. Another cause is the existence of backwater regions little reached so far by science, technology, education, health services, and democratic processes. Yet at least half of world poverty today is contrived by the well-to-do to exploit the poor.

The Northerners – Europeans, Northern Americans, and Japanese – who drink coffee, wear shirts, and ride cars with tires pay prices for them so low that the Brazilian coffee-bean picker, Sri Lankan seamstress, and Indonesian rubber tapper are paid only a few dollars a day. This cruel system is euphemistically called free trade, as in freebooter, freeloader, and free-for-all. Free trade among economic equals is exemplary. Among economic unequals it is exploitation, pure and simple.

AGAIN TIME FOR EMANCIPATION

So far, the human race has not been "very good" at exercising its responsibilities toward global equity, observed medical scientist Lewis Thomas. He said there is nothing "natural or stable about a world society in which two-thirds of the population, and all the children of that two-thirds, have no real chance at human living while those of us who are well off turn our heads away. . . . The only excuse I can make for us is that we are new at the game. . . . We have not yet begun to grow up" and are still in a stage of "juvenile delinquency." Nevertheless, Dr. Thomas stated, "we are genetically programmed for social living," and equity is a moral obligation "driven by deep biological imperatives."

It is long past time for emancipation of the hundreds of millions of persons on earth who are paid only a few dollars a day for their work and whose families are thus enslaved in poverty. The masters of this bondage are industrialized-country business people, consumers, and collaborating developing-country political and business elites. In 1995 the World Summit for Social Development issued the Copenhagen Declaration and Programme of Action, describing poverty in all its aspects and proposing various actions to enable everyone to have at least the bare necessities of life. Hoping for some sort of remedy, United Nations Secretary-General Boutros Boutros-Ghali proclaimed 1996 as the International Year for the Eradication of Poverty. It is expected that the U N General Assembly will designate 1997-2006 as the Decade for the Eradication of Poverty. If we became seriously humane, however, the goal could be realized in half that time. There could again be a great abolition movement and a global emancipation proclamation.

The 1.3 billion persons living in poverty in the world South have an average annual per-capita income equivalent to about $300, a total of close to $400 billion. If their earnings doubled to $600 each, an incremental total of another $400 billion, they could climb out of poverty and just barely meet their basic needs. So let us say that the base incremental amount of money needed annually to end poverty in the global South within four years, that is by the end of year 2000, is $400 billion. Let us also postulate that the possibility of that happening would depend on increasing the income of other Southerners during that period by that amount or more, say $600 billion. Then the total goal would be $1000 billion yearly. This may be compared with the somewhat less sufficient "Agenda 21" program, costing $611 billion annually, presented at the U N Conference on Environment and Development at Rio de Janeiro in 1992.

Where could the enormous amount of $1000 billion of new money or resources come from? I suggest the possibilities of $400 billion from four innovative North-South trade-offs at $100 billion each, $300 billion from an enhanced rate of growth in the South, and $300 billion from increasing the amount of foreign aid to 1.7 percent of the North's gross national product.

NORTH-SOUTH WANTS FROM EACH OTHER

Potential trade-offs can be identified by asking two complementary questions: What does the global North want from the South? What does the South want from the North?

Northerners would like Southerners to have fewer children, to control terrorism and illegal drug supply, to conserve forests and other environments, to continue to export large tonnages of minerals and tropical crops, to open their markets to Northern producers, and to develop their societies more democratically and equitably. These Northern desires, taken together, are very great. If fulfilled on any appreciable scale, they would save the North enormous amounts of money. So it is entirely possible that the North would be willing to offer in return substantial concessions for its share in joint interests and corrective leveling of the playing field in trade and other international relations.

Southerners, for their part, would like Northerners to cancel those parts of Southern debts attributable to Northern monetary purposes, Northerners to pay enough for imports to allow Southern producers a living wage, to reduce trade barriers, to establish a code of conduct for Northern corporations operating in the South, further to abate Northern pollution, and to forego Northern intervention in the domestic affairs of Southern countries.

POTENTIAL NORTH-SOUTH TRADE-OFFS

These respective wants by the North and South provide a realistic opportunity for trade-offs benefitting all. Four plausible trade-offs, each valued at about $100 billion annually, could be arranged:

(1) The South might offer to forego the agricultural and industrial potential income from cutting one billion acres of forest (some one-fifth of the earth's closed forest) at say $100 an acre. The North in return might cancel one-half of the South's international debt. The servicing of that total debt costs approximately $200 billion annually.

(2) Petroleum is substantially underpriced, some analysts recognize, because little or no account is taken of depletion of natural capital, cost of the pollution it causes, and the notably higher costs of alternative liquid fuels. Furthermore, the industrialized North has already used up its per-capita share of the oil originally deposited in the earth's crust. Thus the North is not entitled to any more oil from the Middle East or elsewhere in the South at any price. If the North insists on importing Southern oil well beyond its share, it can be argued that a price supplement should be paid for that privilege. A surcharge of $11 a barrel on 9 billion barrels of crude petroleum (including crude equivalent of refined products) exported from South to North yearly would yield $100 billion.

(3) Minerals (other than petroleum) and agricultural commodities exported from South to North are similarly underpriced. The reason, again, is partly absence of consideration of depletion of natural capital. The clearest indicator of inadequacy of price is the low wage (often $1 a day to unskilled workers) paid to the farmers and laborers producing the commodities. If an import tax doubled the price on Southern commodity exports and a 25-percent decline in volume due to the higher prices were figured in, some $100 billion would be available for poverty reduction.

(4) Northern trade barriers cost the South about $200 billion a year in trade. If the North abolished half of those barriers, Southerners would earn $100 billion additional annually to help raise wages to modest minimums. Such action would mean drastic occupational shifts in the North. So it could happen only if the

South offered as a trade-off what is probably the North's greatest want from it – effective slowdown in global population growth. In fact, the North might also reasonably insist on appreciably Southern advances in equal rights for women, land reform, and democracy.

These four trade-offs could provide the $400 billion a year needed to enable Southerners to earn their way out of poverty. The complementary benefits to Northerners would be equally rewarding. The feasibility of generating wherewithal this way is enhanced by the fact that none of it would come from hard-pressed national budgets. Nor would any of it come from demands on present wealth. It would flow from more equitable practices in trade and financial transactions and a fairer distribution of future earnings.

The trade-offs could be negotiated by the reorganized United Nations Security and Development Council. Funds generated by the trade-offs could be placed in a Southern Development Fund (SDF) managed by Southern representatives with advice and consent of the Council. Allocations from the SDF would go principally to increase the opportunities and returns to those in poverty. They would mainly increase commodity prices (at the farm or mine level) and substandard wages. Additionally they would finance agricultural inputs, farm-to-market roads, clinics, and schools.

HIGHER GROWTH RATES

Another source of incremental funds to eliminate poverty would be higher growth rates. The United Nations analysis published in *Global Outlook 2000* reported that a conventional baseline forecast for the rate of growth of gross domestic product (GDP) in the South during 1990-2000 was 4.3 percent annually. It further said that three economic models indicated that more enlightened policies during the period could boost the Southern growth rate to between 5 and 6 percent. The baseline rate of growth, 4.3 percent, would raise the South's GDP from $4.1 trillion in 1994 to $5.3 trillion in 2000. However a possible alternative growth rate of, say 5.3 percent, would yield a GDP of $5.6 trillion in 2000, an increment of $300 billion. The enlightened policies making that possible would be improvements in two practices involved in the previously-mentioned trade-offs – debt reduction and lower Northern trade protection; another policy to be noted next – greater foreign aid; and additionally the factors of greater Southern savings, Northern economic growth, and worldwide reduction in armaments trade.

FOREIGN AID

A third source of incremental funds for the South to help eliminate poverty would be an increased sense of responsibility by well-to-do people to erect a sufficient global safety net for those of humanity who so far have been greatly disadvantaged. The industrialized nations belonging to the Organization for Economic Cooperation and Development (OECD) contributed 0.3 percent of their GNP to foreign aid (official development assistance – ODA) in 1993. That compares with goals of 0.7 percent proposed by the United Nations in 1961 and of 1.0 percent recommended by economist Jan Tinbergen in 1976. If OECD increased its ODA to the still modest share of 1.7 percent of its GNP by year 2000, it would add $300 billion annually above the 1993 amount of $54 billion.

BETTER PROGRAMMING

Good budgeting entails, of course, not only adequate receipts but also prudent expenditure patterns. Where primary goals are poverty elimination and more equal opportunity , this means restructuring toward higher than usual expenditure priorities for agricultural extension and research, primary and vocational education, low-cost housing, and health services. Simultaneously it means lower priorities for armaments, debt servicing (made possible by such trade-offs as previously suggested), and big power and transportation projects. A movement to rid developing countries of their armies is being led by Oscar Arias, former president of Costa Rica, and other Nobel Prize winners.

Yet management of funds is only one part of poverty elimination. Successful strategies to allow the poor to lift themselves include providing equal services to women, taxing family agriculture lightly,

Table 2
Baseline and Alternative Gross Domestic Product in Global South in Year 2000, by Sectors
(In U.S. $ 1994 billion)

Sector	2000 base line	Re-struc-turing	2000 alter-native
BASIC HUMAN NEEDS:			
Food	1696	108	1804
Housing	318	100	418
Clothing	265	18	283
Water and home sanitation	159	11	170
Fuel and home power	159	9	168
Health	239	41	280
Education	228	149	377
Conservation of air, water, land, forests, and fisheries	16	10	26
Subtotal basic needs	3080	446	3526
EXTRA GOODS AND SERVICES:			
Transportation and communication	418	3	421
Convenient goods and services, not elsewhere classified	1150	120	1270
Military	254	– 161	93
Debt servicing, international	233	– 147	86
Government, not elsewhere classif.	159	23	182
Energy and mineral conservation	6	16	22
Subtotal extra goods and serv.	2220	– 146	2074
Grand total	5300	300	5600

Sources: Modified from U. N., World Bank, and other agencies.

encouraging volunteer workers, arranging joint liability instead of collateral for small loans, building farm-to-market roads, distributing health services through clinics only the poor are likely to attend, and subsidizing those foods consumed mainly by low-income peoples. Within sectors, fairness to the poor calls for such emphases as primary education, preventive health care, family planning for children, and agriculture for the domestic market. See Table 2.

Hundreds of significant books have been published about development in the South. Particularly recommended are the following dozen analysts (see Reference section for titles of their books): Brecher on enlightened policies, Haq on ethics and meaningful statistics, Prosterman on best programs, Meadows on forecasts and sustainability, Brown and Turner on the environment, Durning on grass-roots participation, Piel on science and population, Goldemberg on energy, and Schumacher, Henderson, and Daly on humane economics.

THE ENVIRONMENT

Restructuring to bring the global environment into sustainable balance by the year 2000 would require just about as much in comprehensive strategies and political will as poverty elimination. However, the funds called for would be a whole order of magnitude smaller, apparently an increment of some $100 billion annually beyond present expenditures.

With regard to the Southern demisphere, it is fortuitous that most of the needed environmental strategies coincide with the poverty strategies and thus do not need additional funds, work, or materials. This applies particularly to soil conservation, water purification, reforestation, and population stabilization.

PROGRESS IS OF THE SPIRIT

This book has tried to describe what a fairer world would look like and the most pragmatic ways to get there. We shall not proceed along the constructive journey unless we have sufficient motivation. So the proposed trade-offs and other suggestions have focused on hopefully tempting rewards. Yet there is more to life than having one's material wants satisfied. It becomes clear when we ponder a real definition of progress by the late Unitarian minister A. Powell Davies:

"Whatever dwells within the mystery of human life is demanding – demanding at all costs – that human life improve its quality. That is what progress is. Not the mere multiplication of comfort and convenience. Not prosperity. Not even security. But insight and wisdom and character; the elimination of greed and the lust for power; the coming of love and unselfishness to dominance. . . . Progress, therefore must mean a deepening of truth and an unfaltering fidelity to it in all human affairs; progress must mean justice, not merely as an aspiration but in embodiment; and progress must mean not the debasement of life and defacement of the earth to serve rapacity and avarice, but beauty; life's loveliness adored and worshiped and carried toward perfection. Progress is of the spirit."

So it is hoped we are poised to usher in a fairer world. The crucial Northern responsibility is to initiate the comprehensive dialogues toward constitutional reform and equal international trade-offs. The choice to be made by the world's well-to-do was defined by Adlai E. Stevenson, in his A. Powell Davies Memorial Lecture in Washington in 1959: "We can use our wealth, our capacity for some vision of truth, some ideal of brotherhood, or we can imprison ourselves within the selfishness of our own concerns and the limitations of a narrow nationhood."

Davies himself – a scholar, mystic, and clergyman – six years before, as quoted by Justice William O. Douglas, had identified the priorities and the challenge: "We must become, throughout the world, the revolutionaries of liberty, and of justice without which liberty is a mockery; revolutionaries of equality, the equality throughout the world of human opportunity; and of unity, the unity of all the world, involved at last within a common destiny. . . . The future belongs to the free peoples if they are willing to deserve it; and to deserve it they must share it."

REFERENCES

Amy, Douglas J., *Real Choices / New Voices*: The Case for Proportional Representation Elections in the United States, Columbia University Press, New York, 1993.

Anner, John, "Community Safety & Police Accountability," *Z Magazine*, July/Aug. 1995.

Associated Press, "Fiscal Health of States Is Strong, Study Finds," *Washington Post*, Nov. 8, 1995.

Associated Press, "Clinton Approves Intelligence Spending Rise," *Washington Post*, Oct. 12, 1996.

Balz, Dan, "GOP Governors Seek Shift in Power," *Washington Post*, Nov. 21, 1994.

Balz, Dan, and Brownstein, Ronald, "God's Fixer," *Washington Post Magazine*, Jan. 28, 1986.

Barbash, Fred, "Britain's 'Privatized' Parliament," London despatch, *Washington Post*, Feb. 3, 1995.

Barbash, Fred, "The Movement to Rule Britannia Differently - Popularity Grows for Written Constitution, Bill of Rights, Senate-Like Chamber," London despatch, *Washington Post*, Sept. 23, 1995.

Barnet, Richard J., and Cavanagh, John, *Global Dreams*: Imperial Corporations and the New World Order, Simon & Schuster, New York, 1994.

Beer, Samuel H., *To Make A Nation*: The Rediscovery of American Federalism, Belknap Press of Harvard University Press, Cambridge, Mass., 1993.

Bernstein, Richard B., with Agel, Jerome, *Amending America*: If We Love the Constitution So Much, Why Do We Keep Trying to Change It?, Times Books, a Division of Random House, New York, 1993.

Berry, Mary Frances, *Why ERA Failed*: Politics, Women's Rights, and the Amending Process of the Constitution, Indiana University Press, Bloomington and Indianapolis, 1986.

Blair, Bruce G., "Who's Got the Button?", *Washington Post*, Sept. 29, 1996.

Block, Fred, "Toward Real Corporate Responsibility," *In These Times*, May 27, 1996.

Boyte, Harry C., "Reinventing Citizenship," *Kettering Review*, winter 1994.

Bradley, Senator Bill, *Time Present, Time Past*: A Memoir, Alfred A. Knopf, New York, 1996.

Brecher, Jeremy; Childs, John Brown; and Cutler, Jill (eds.), *Global Visions*: Beyond the New World Order, South End Press, Boston, 1993.

Brennan, Justice William J., Jr., "As He Turns 90, Brennan Criticizes Death Penalty," Associated Press, *Washington Post*, Apr. 28, 1996.

Broder, David S., "Democracy by Poll," *Washington Post*, Apr. 25, 1994.

Broder, David S., "The Citizenship Movement," *Washington Post*, Nov. 27, 1994.

Brown, Lester, et al., *State of the World 1996*, Worldwatch Institute(Washington), W. W. Norton, New York, 1996.

Bryan, Kathy, "Mend It, Don't End It: The Affirmative Action Debate," *AAUW Outlook* (American Association of University Women), fall 1996.

Clark, Grenville, and Sohn, Louis B., *World Peace Through World Law*, Harvard University Press, Cambridge, Mass., 1966 (3rd ed.enlarged).

Clarke, Tony et al., *Dismantling Corporate Rule*: Toward a New Form of Politics in an Age of Globalization, Working Committee onTCNs, International Forum on Globalization, San Francisco, 1996.

Claude, Inis L., *States and the Global System*: Politics, Law, and Organization, St. Martin's Press, New York, 1988.

Claybrook, Joan, *Miami Herald*, Mar. 4, 1990.

Commission on Global Governance, *Our Global Neighborhood*, Oxford University Press, New York, 1995.

Daly, Herman E., and Cobb, Jr., John B., *For the Common Good*: Redirecting the Economy Toward Community, the Environment, and a Sustainable Future, Beacon Press, Boston, 1989.

Danaher, Kevin (ed.), *Fifty Years Is Enough*: The Case Against the World Bank & International Monetary Fund, South End Press, Boston, 1994.

Davies, Ernest Albert John, "Public Utilities," *Encyclopaedia Britannica*, University of Chicago, Chicago, vol. 18, p. 835-840.

De Soto, Hernando, *The Other Path*: The Invisible Revolution in the Third World, Harper & Row, New York, 1990.

Devroy, Ann, and Dewar, Helen, "Hailing Bipartianship, Clinton Signs Bill to Restrict Unfunded Mandates," *Washington Post*, Mar. 23, 1995.

Dionne, E. J., Jr., "Democracy or Plutocracy?," *Washington Post*, Feb. 15, 1994.

Dionne, E. J., Jr., "To the Governors (Again)," *Washington Post*, Dec. 13, 1994.

Douglas, William O. (ed.), *The Mind and Faith of A. Powell Davies*, Doubleday & Co., Garden City, NY, 1959, p. 186.

Douthwaite, Richard, *The Growth Illusion*: How Economic Growth Has Enriched the Few, Impoverished the Many, and Endangered the Planet, Council Oak Books, Tulsa, Okla., 1992.

Drozdiak, William, "Regions on the Rise: As European Borders Become More Porous, Cities Replace Countries in Transnational Economic Alliances," *Washington Post*, Oct. 22, 1995.

Dugger, Ronnie, "Real Populists Please Stand Up: A Call to Citizens," *The Nation*, Aug. 14/21, 1995, p. 159-164.

Durning, Alan B., *Poverty and the Environment*: Reversing the Downward Spiral, Paper 92, Worldwatch Institute, Washington, 1989.

Edsall, Thomas B., "Public Grows More Receptive to Anti-Government Message," *Washington Post*, Jan. 31, 1996.

Eggers, William D., and O'Leary, John, *Revolution at the Roots*: Making Our Government Smaller, Better, and Closer to Home, The Free Press, New York, 1995.

Estes, Ralph, *Tyranny of the Bottom Line*: Why Corporations Make Good People Do Bad Things, Berrett-Koehler Publishers, San Francisco, 1996.

Etzioni, Amitai, *The Spirit of Community*: The Reinvention of American Society, Simon & Schuster, New York, 1993.

Falk, Richard, *Explorations at the Edge of Time*: The Prospects for World Order, Temple University Press, Philadelphia, 1992.

Fishkin, James S., *Democracy and Deliberation*: New Directions for Democratic Reform, Yale University Press, New Haven, 1991.

Fishkin, James S., *The Voice of the People*: Public Opinion and Democracy, Yale University Press, New Haven, 1995.

Fraser, Steve, and Lichtenstein, Nelson, "New Life for the Labor Movement," *Washington Post*, Dec. 31, 1995.

Freedom House, "The Map of Freedom - 1996," *Freedom Review*, Jan. - Feb. 1996, p. 39-41.

Freeman, Richard, and Rogers, Joel, as reported by Frank Swoboda, *Washington Post*, Dec. 6, 1994.

Gans, Herbert J., *The War Against the Poor*: The Underclass and Antipoverty Policy, BasicBooks, a division of HarperCollins Publishers, New York, 1995.

Gellner, Ernest, *Conditions of Liberty*: Civil Society and Its Rivals, Allan Lane/The Penguin Press, London, 1994.

Giancaterino, Randy, "The National Executive Service Corps," *Prime Times* (National Association for Retired Credit Union People), March 1995.

Ginsberg, M., "Social Philosophy," *Encyclopaedia Britannica*, University of Chicago, vol. 20, 1943.

Glossop, Ronald J., *World Federation?*: A Critical Analysis of Federal World Government, McFarland & Co., Publishers, Jefferson, NC and London, 1993.

Goldemberg, Jose, et al., *Energy for a Sustainable World*, Wiley Eastern Limited, New Delhi, 1988. Extended excerpts in Energy for Development, World Resources Institute, Washington, and Oxford & IBH Publishing Co. Pvt. Ltd., New Delhi.

Goldman, Ralph M. (ed.), *Transnational Parties*: Organizing the World's Precincts, University Press of America, Lanham, Md., 1883.

Gordon, David M., "Underpaid Workers, Bloated Corporations: Two Pieces in the Puzzle of U. S. Economic Decline," *Dissent*, spring 1996, p. 23-34.

Green, John Richard, "A Short History of the English People," *The World's Great Classics*, vol. III, The Colonial Press, New York, 1900 (rev. ed.)

Gugliotta, Guy, "Scaling Down the American Dream," *Washington Post*, Apr. 19, 1995.

Guizot, Francois Pierre Guillaume, "History of Civilization in Europe," translated by William Hazlitt, *The World's Great Classics*, vol. III, The Colonial Press, New York, 1900 (rev. ed.)

Haq, Mahbub ul (project director), et al., *Human Development Report*, United Nations Development Programme, Oxford University Press, New York, annually.

Harris, Errol E., *One World or None*: Prescription for Survival, Humanities Press, Atlantic Highlands, NJ, 1993.

Hatter, Terry. U. S. District Judge Terry Hatter of Los Angeles is quoted by Mary Pat Flaherty and Juan Biskupic, "Rules Often Impose Toughest Penalties on Poor, Minorities," *Washington Post*, Oct. 9, 1996.

Havemann, Judith, "Scholars Question Whether Welfare Shift Is Reform," *Washington Post*, Apr. 20, 1995.

Henderson, Hazel, *The Politics of the Solar Age*: Alternatives to Economics, Knowledge Systems, Indianapolis, IN, 1988 (rev. ed.)

Herbert, Wray, "The Revival of Civic Life," *U.S. News & World Report*, Jan. 29, 1996.

Hutton, Will, *The State We're In*, Vintage, London, 1996 (rev. ed.)

Hyneman, Charles S., and Carey, George W., *A Second Federalist*: Congress Creates a Government, University of South Carolina Press, Columbia, S.C., 1967.

In These Times, "Americans Support the Militia's Devil," editorial, July 10, 1995.

In These Times, "An Alternative Democratic Platform," Sept. 2, 1996.

Independent Progressive Politics Network, "Common Platform of the National Slate of Independent Progressive Candidates," 1996.

Irwin, David, "Town Meeting Icon of Odd Evolution," *Laconia (NH) Evening Citizen*, Aug. 24, 1995.

Jefferson, Thomas. Quotation is from letter to William Charles Jarvis, September 28, 1820 in Paul Leicester Ford (ed.), *The Writings of Thomas Jefferson*, vol. 10, G. P. Putnam's Sons, New York, 1899.

Keefe, William J., *Parties, Politics, and Public Policy in America*, Congressional Quarterly Press, Washington, 1991 (6th ed.)

Kenworthy, Tom, "'Green Scissors' Coalition Seeks $33 Billion in Cuts," *Washington Post*, Jan. 31, 1995.

Korten, David C., *When Corporations Rule the World*, Kumarian Press and Berrett-Koehler Publishers, West Hartford, Conn. and San Francisco, 1995.

Lappe, Frances Moore, and Dubois, Paul Martin, *The Quickening of America*: Rebuilding Our Nation, Remaking Our Lives, Jossey-Bass, Inc., Publishers, San Francisco, 1994.

Laursen, Eric, "A Tale of Two Communities: Behind the Privatization Revolution," *Z Magazine*, Oct. 1996.

Lazare, Daniel, *The Frozen Republic*: How the Constitution Is Paralyzing Democracy, Harcourt Brace, 1996.

Lee, Gary, "Report Urges Shift in EPA Authority to States, Firms," *Washington Post*, Apr. 13, 1995.

Leitner, Jane Elligett (chair), *Illustrative Constitution for a Union of NATO, EC, OECD AND CSCE Democracies*, Association to Unite the Democracies, Washington, 1990.

Levine, Arthur, in "Poll Finds College Students Ready to Make a Difference" by Alice Dembner, *Boston Globe*, Sept. 4, 1994.

Lewis, Charles, and The Center for Public Integrity, *The Buying of the President*, Avon Books, New York, 1996.

Liacos, Paul J. See Good, Andrew, "The Lessons of Liacos," *Boston Globe*, July 7, 1996.

Liberal Democrats, *"We, The People . . .*: Towards a Written Constitution, Federal Green Paper No. 13, Hebden Royd Publications, Ltd., London.

Lind, Michael, *The Next American Nation*: The New Nationalism and the Fourth American Revolution, Free Press, New York, 1995.

Locke, John, *Two Treatises of Government*, 1690. Reprinted with introduction by William S. Carpenter, Everyman's Library, J. M. Dent & Sons Ltd., London and E. P. Dutton & Co., Inc., New York, 1924.

Makhijani, Arjun, "U. S. Nuclear Waste Program in Crisis," interview by Francis Macy (ed.), *Nuclear Guardianship Forum* (Berkeley, CA), Issue 3, spring 1994.

Malone, Dumas (ed.), "James Wilson," *Dictionary of American Biography*, Charles Scribner's Sons, New York, 1943, vol. 20.

Manglapus, Raul S., "Human Rights Are Not a Western Discovery," *Worldview* (Council on Religion and International Affairs), Oct. 1978.

Marcus, Ruth, "High Court Curbing Companies,"
Washington Post, Apr. 5, 1990.

Marr, Andrew, *Ruling Britannia*: The Failure and Future of British
Democracy, Michael Joseph, London, 1995.

Mathews, David, *Politics for People*: Finding a Responsible Public Voice,
University of Illinois Press, Urbana, 1994.

Matthews, Allan F., "Attack on World Poverty: What Are the Major
Obstacles to Worldwide Equality of Opportunity?," *The Minority of One*
(Passaic, NJ), Dec. 1964.

Matthews, Allan F., "The People United: Reclaiming Sovereignty and
Globalizing from Below," *Toward Freedom* (Burlington, VT),
Aug./Sept. 1995.

McLaughlin, Andrew, *Constitutional History of the United States*, Appleton
Century, New York, 1936.

Meadows, Donella H.; Meadows, Dennis L.; and Randers, Jorgen, *Beyond
the Limits*: Confronting Global Collapse, Envisioning a Sustainable
Future, Chelsea Green Publishing Co., Post Mills, Vermont, 1992.

Meeker-Lowry, Susan, "The Potential of Local Currency,"
Z Magazine, July/Aug. 1995.

Merida, Kevin, "Americans Want a Direct Say in Political Decision-
Making, Pollsters Find," *Washington Post*, Apr. 20, 1994.

Morgan, Edmund S., *Inventing the People*: The Rise of Popular Sovereignty
in England and America, Norton, New York, 1988.

Morris, Scott M., review of book by Wendell Berry in *Washington Post Book
World*, Jan. 21, 1996.

Mueller, Dennis C., *Constitutional Democracy*, Oxford University Press,
New York, 1996.

Nader, Ralph; Green, Mark; and Seligman, Joel, *Taming the Giant
Corporation*, W. W. Norton, New York, 1976.

Nader, Ralph, et al., *The Case Against "Free Trade"*: GATT, NAFTA, and
the Globalization of Corporate Power, Earth Island Press, North
Atlantic Books, San Francisco, 1993.

Nash, Roderick Frazier, *The Rights of Nature*: A History of Environmental
Ethics, University of Wisconsin Press, Madison, Wis., 1989.

Nettels, Curtis P., *The Roots of American Civilization*: A History of American
Colonial Life, Appleton-Century-Crofts, Inc., New York, 1938.

New Party National Committee, "New Party Principles,"
   New Party News, spring 1996.

New York Times, "Toward a More Perfect Union," editorial, July 8, 1962,

Nichols, Hank, "Why Not Just Abolish Congress and Dial Our Vote by
   Computer," *Boston Globe*, Aug. 28, 1994.

Nicholson, Marlene A., "Financing Political Speech," *in The Oxford
   Companion to The Supreme Court of the United States* by Kermit L. Hall
   (ed.), Oxford University Press, New York and Oxford, 1992.

Oldenburg, Ray, *The Great Good Places*: Cafes, Coffee Shops, Community
   Centers, Beauty Parlors, General Stores, Bars, Hangouts, and How
   They Get You Through the Day, Paragon House, Santa Rosa, Calif.,
   1989.

Paine, Thomas, *Rights of Man*, 1791-92. Reprinted by Penguin Books, with
   introduction by Eric Foner, New York and London, 1969/1984/1985.

Peters, William, *A More Perfect Union*, Crown Publishers,
   New York, 1987.

Philips, Kevin, *Arrogant Capital*: Washington, Wall Street, and the
   Frustration of American Politics, Little, Brown and Co., Boston, 1994.

Piel, Gerard, *Only One World*: Our Own to Make and Keep, W. H.
   Freeman and Co., New York, 1992.

Pinder, John, *European Community*: The Building of a Union, Oxford
   University Press, Oxford, 1995 (2nd ed.).

Pope, Carl, "A Tale of Two Countries," advertisement,
   Washington Post, Oct. 6, 1994.

Prosterman, Roy L., and Riedinger, Jeffrey M., *Land Reform and Democratic
   Development*, Johns Hopkins University Press, Baltimore, 1987.

Raspberry, William, "The Separation of Power from the People,"
   Washington Post, May 8, 1995.

Reich, Charles A., *Opposing the System*, Crown Publishers, Inc.,
   New York, 1995.

Rivlin, Alice M., *Reviving the American Dream*: The Economy, the States &
   the Federal Government, The Brookings Institution,
   Washington, 1992.

Roberts, Justice Owen J.; Schmidt, John F.; and Streit, Clarence K.,
   The New Federalist, Harper & Brothers, Publishers, New York, 1950.

Rogers, Joel. See reference by Weinstein.

Ross, Warren A., "Are You a Communitarian Without Knowing It," *World* (Unitarian Universalist Association), Sept./Oct. 1994.

Rowan, Carl T., "Back to 'State's Rights,'" *Washington Post*, Nov. 5, 1995.

Sandel, Michael J., *Democracy's Discontent*: America in Search of a Public Philosophy, Harvard University Press, Cambridge, Mass., 1996.

Schmidt, David D., *Citizen Lawmakers*: The Ballot Initiative Revolution, Temple University Press, Philadelphia, 1989.

Schmidt, Susan, "Threats to U. S. Agents on Public Lands Detailed," *Washington Post*, May 10, 1995.

Schumacher, E. F., *Small Is Beautiful*: Economics As If People Mattered, Blond & Briggs, Ltd., London; Harper & Row, New York, 1973.

Selby, John E., *The Revolution in Virginia 1775-1783*, The Colonial Williamsburg Foundation, Williamsburg, Va., 1988.

Selden, Harry Louis, "The Electoral College: Does It Choose the Best Man?", *American Heritage*, Oct. 1962.

Shapiro, Robert J., "End Corporate Welfare," *Washington Post*, Dec. 1, 1995.

Sivard, Ruth Leger, *World Military and Social Expenditures 1996*, World Priorities, Washington, 1996.

Spinelli, Altiero, *Speeches in European Parliament 1976-1986*, edited by Pier Virgilio Dastoli, Communist and Allies Group - European Parliament, Bruxelles, 1986.

Stillman, Bradley, "Looser Media Ownership Rules Pressed" by Mike Mille and Paul Farhi, *Washington Post*, Dec. 5, 1995.

Streit, Clarence K., *Union Now*: A Proposal for a Federal Union of Democracies of the North Atlantic, Harper & Brothers Publishers, New York, 1939.

Sundquist, James L., *Constitutional Reform and Effective Government*, Brookings Institution, Washington, 1992 (rev. ed.).

Szent-Miklosy, Istvan, *The Atlantic Union Movement*: Its Significance in World Politics, Fountainhead Publishers, New York, 1965.

Theobald, Robert. See William Raspberry, "In A Dangerous Sea Together," *Washington Post*, Sept. 27, 1996. Also Theobald's forthcoming book, *Reworking Success*.

Thomas, Lewis, *The Fragile Species*, Collier Books, Macmillan Publishing Co., New York, 1992.

Thurow, Lester, "The Crusade That's Killing Prosperity,"
   American Prospect, March-April 1996.

Time-Life Books, Inc., *Fury of the Northmen, Time Frame AD 800-1000*,
   Alexandria, Va., 1988.

Times Mirror Center for the People & the Press, in "Redefining the
   Middle: A Worried Bloc of Voters Seeking an Alternative" by David S.
   Broder, *Washington Post*, Sept. 21, 1994.

Tinbergen, Jan (coordinator), *RIO - Reshaping the International Order*: A
   Report to the Club of Rome, A Signet Book, New American Library,
   New York, 1976.

Truman, Harry S. His comment on the CIA was in the *Washington Post*,
   Dec. 22, 1963.

Turner II, B. L. (ed.) et al., *The Earth As Transformed by Human Action*:
   Global and Regional Changes in the Biosphere over the Past 300 Years,
   Cambridge University Press, New York, 1990.

United Nations, *World Summit for Social Development 6-12 March 1995*:
   The Copenhagen Declaration and Programme of Action,
   New York, 1995.

United Nations, *Global Outlook 2000*: An Economic, Social and
   Environmental Perspective, U. N., New York, 1990.

United Nations Conference on Environment and Development, Earth
   Summit *Agenda 21*: The U N Programme of Action from Rio,
   Department of Public Information, U N, New York, 1993.

United Nations Development Programme, *Human Development Report*,
   Oxford University Press, New York and Oxford, 1994.

U. S. News & World Report, "The New America - A New U. S. News Poll
   Shatters Old Assumptions About American Politics," July 10, 1995.

Warsh, David, "Needed: A Lobby for Labor, Like the AARP,"
   Boston Globe, Sept. 3, 1995.

Washington Post, "A Fetid System," editorial, Aug. 15, 1995.

Weinstein, James, "In the Trenches - The New Party looks to build an
   urban-oriented political movement from the ground up,"
   In These Times, July 22, 1996.

Wertheimer, Fred, Newsweek, Nov. 14, 1988, p. 22. "The Capitol's Capital
   Scandal," *Washington Post*, Mar. 22, 1992.

Wolff, Edward N., "Time for a Wealth Tax?", *The Boston Review*,
   Feb./Mar. 1996.

Wood, Christopher A., "The War for Western Lands," *Washington Post*, May 7, 1995.

World Almanac, "Nations of the World," *The World Almanac and Book of Facts 1996*, Funk & Wagnals Corp., Mahwah, NJ, 1995.

Yankelovich, Daniel, and Harman, Sidney, *Starting with the People*, Houghton Mifflin Co., Boston, 1988.

Yankelovich, Daniel, *Coming to Public Judgment*: Making Democracy Work in a Complex World, Syracuse University Press, Syracuse, NY, 1991.

INDEX

ABOUT THE AUTHOR

Allan Matthews, the author, lived as a youngster in rural south-eastern Pennsylvania, majored in geology during college years in the Middle West, and has lived mainly in northern Virginia suburbs of Washington, DC. Summers were often close to his family roots in Gilford, New Hampshire. His principal career was helping to program United States public cooperation in the development of Africa and southern Arabia. This included living several years in Liberia and Yemen. He is secretary of the Association to Unite the Democracies.

WHERE TO ORDER BOOK

Copies of this book are available for $8 prepaid (including handling and shipping) from Sovereign People Press, P. O. Box 8332, Reston, VA 20195-2132. For this small edition, fulfillment of orders will generally be limited to three copies per buyer. Consideration may be given under special circumstances to requests for somewhat larger orders, but the quoted price leaves no room for discounts on quantity purchases. Telephone (703) 435-5093.